OPEN UP
ALICE CASEY

WESTBOW
PRESS®
A DIVISION OF THOMAS NELSON
& ZONDERVAN

Copyright © 2019 Alice Casey.

All rights reserved. No part of this book may be used or reproduced by any means, graphic, electronic, or mechanical, including photocopying, recording, taping or by any information storage retrieval system without the written permission of the author except in the case of brief quotations embodied in critical articles and reviews.

WestBow Press books may be ordered through booksellers or by contacting:

WestBow Press
A Division of Thomas Nelson & Zondervan
1663 Liberty Drive
Bloomington, IN 47403
www.westbowpress.com
1 (866) 928-1240

Because of the dynamic nature of the Internet, any web addresses or links contained in this book may have changed since publication and may no longer be valid. The views expressed in this work are solely those of the author and do not necessarily reflect the views of the publisher, and the publisher hereby disclaims any responsibility for them.

Any people depicted in stock imagery provided by Getty Images are models, and such images are being used for illustrative purposes only. Certain stock imagery © Getty Images.

ISBN: 978-1-9736-5779-8 (sc)
ISBN: 978-1-9736-5781-1 (hc)
ISBN: 978-1-9736-5780-4 (e)

Library of Congress Control Number: 2019903401

Print information available on the last page.

WestBow Press rev. date: 4/9/2019

The List

1	Ode To A Friend	Sep 24/18
3	A Moment With Christ	Sep 29/18
6	Light in the Storm	Sep 29/18
8	Free Space	Oct 5/18
10	Calling Stars	Oct 5/18
13	To Set Us Free	Oct 5/18
17	Not So Small	Oct 8/18
20	Life Journey	Oct 8/18
22	The Chimes of Stillness	Oct 18/18
23	New Owner	Oct 23/18
26	Night Beats	Oct 23/18
27	Long Lost	Nov 1/18
28	Wings on Air	Nov 9/18
29	Embraced	Nov 10/18
31	Mountain Reflection	Nov 12/18
32	The Word	Nov 14/18
33	Their Cross	Nov 14/18
35	After-Sounds	Nov 16/18
36	Open Road	Nov 18/18
37	Rebound	Nov 18/18
38	Sights and Sounds	Nov 18/18
39	Touched	Nov 18/18
40	The Prayer	Nov 20/18
41	On The Inside	Nov 20/18
42	Communion	Nov 20/18
43	Heart Strings	Nov 21/18
45	Birds in Flight	Nov 21/18
46	Moving On	Nov 22/18
47	Strength of Heart	Nov 22/18
48	That Time of Year	Nov 23/18
50	Aglow	Nov 24/18
51	Washed and Renewed	Nov 25/18
52	Sacred Sunday	Nov 25/18
53	Unstuck	Nov 26/18
54	Almost There	Dec 3/18

55	Encompass Us	Dec 5/18
56	Petitions of Grace	Dec 6/18
57	Distant Dreams	Dec 5/18
58	This Time	Dec 7/18
59	Christmas Ties	Dec 7/18
60	Rising Time	Dec 9/18
61	Put In Place	Dec 9/18
62	Consider Us	Dec 10/18
65	Hold My Hand	Dec 10/18
67	In Search of Joy	Dec 11/18
68	Of The Sea	Dec 12/18
69	Born To Reside	Dec 13/18
70	Springs To Life	Dec 14/18
71	Formless	Dec 16/18
72	The Claws of The Lion	Dec 16/18
73	Letting Go	Dec 18/18
74	It's OK To Cry	Dec 19/18
75	Your Host	Dec 19/18
76	The Devil's Tails	Dec 20/18
77	Elemental in Nature	Dec 20/18
80	Poetically Just	Dec 21/18
81	Good as Gold	Dec 21/18
82	Selah	Dec 21/18
84	The Published Soul	Dec 22/18
85	Curtan Calls	Dec 22/18
86	Joyful Boy	Dec 22/18
87	Unflappable	Dec 22/18
90	The Vibration of Christ	Dec 23/18
91	Afflicted	Dec 23/18
92	For The Good Times	Dec 23/18
97	Fair of Feather	Dec 24/18
98	The God Release	Dec 24/18
99	In God's Name	Dec 25/18
100	The Clearing	Dec 26/18
102	Through The Trees	Dec 26/18
104	Tastes To See	Dec 26/18
105	The Messenger	Dec 27/18

108	The Interval	Dec 27/18
109	Read Between The Lines	Dec 27/18
110	Close The Books	Dec 27/18
111	Land of Grand	Dec 27/18
114	Merchant's Deceits	Dec 28/18
115	The Potter	Dec 28/18
116	Coincidentally	Dec 29/18
117	Specialist of Light	Dec 29/18
118	Action Moves	Dec 30/18
120	Deeper Waters	Dec 30/18
121	Lifestream	Dec 31/18
122	Light Switch	Dec 31/18
123	Cleansing Time	Dec 31/18
124	Gifts of Reason	Dec 31/18
125	The New Recruits	Jan 1/19
126	The Plaintive Calls	Jan 1/19
127	Glow With Christ	Jan 1/19
128	In The Name Of God	Jan 1/19
129	Imprints	Jan 1/19
130	Lasting Impressions	Jan 2/19
131	Take Them In	Jan 2/19
132	Words of Play	Jan 2/19
133	Foods For Life	Jan 2/19
134	The Uniforms	Jan 3/19
135	Tried and True	Jan 3/19
136	Just Shout Hallelujah	Jan 3/19
139	Just Go To God	Jan 3/19
140	Red Flags	Jan 4/19
141	The Unspoken Word	Jan 4/19
142	War Games	Jan 4/19
145	Have Faith	Jan 5/19
146	Look At My Face	Jan 5/19
147	It's My Party	Jan 5/19
148	Connections	Jan 5/19
149	Overflows	Jan 5/19
150	The Bully's Points	Jan 6/19
152	In God's Good Time	Jan 7/19

153	Tempest's Brew	Jan 10/19
155	Come In	Jan 1/19
156	Artificial Flavors	Jan 13/19
157	Pretty Colors	Jan 13/19
158	Set In Place	Jan 15/19
160	The Reason	Jan 15/19
161	Empty Spaces	Jan 17/19
162	Passing Ships	Jan 17/19
163	In His Grace	Jan 18/19
164	Good God	Jan 18/19
165	Relocation	Jan 21/19
166	Dream Intents	Jan 21/19
167	Reunite	Jan 21/19
168	Get Real	Jan 21/19

Introduction

I give thanks to my Maker. I owe it to Him, although asks for no payment from me. I owe it to the memory of my loved ones. I believe they will know my appreciation on another level – a deeper level, because they are no longer separated by the guard and veil of ego, the grand divide to the eyes of love and truth.

I have come to feel and realize the impact of God's Holy Spirit in His words of His great book, the Bible, where He says He takes the weak things in this world, and strengthens them, and makes them the chief cornerstone; (2 Corinthians 13:9) and to not be ashamed of our weaknesses, because when we are weak, then He is strong (2 Corinthians 12:10) - what others have cast aside He will use for the best and most worthy purposes, and says .....Yes, I will strengthen thee; (Isaiah 41:10) that all things are possible, where with men this is impossible; but with God all things are possible. (Matthew 19:26) He tells us to knock and we will find the opening. (Matthew 7:7)

There are so many passages I am finding, both literally and figuratively with God. He lightens my world – my most heavy loads and He will still continue to carry them: He never stops. In Deuteronomy 31:6, He tells us, "Be strong and of a good courage, fear not, nor be afraid of them: for the Lord thy God, it is he that doth go with thee: he will not fail thee, nor forsake thee." He reassures us by telling us that He loves us with an everlasting love – how great is that! How can I not thank Him?

He tells us His burden is light....He does make it so when He walks with me. I just bought a pedometer because they say one should aim to do 10,000 steps per day for the healthiest benefits – that's what we should strive for; so I will begin that journey one step at a time.

I really have so many things to say about that journey – about this God. I feel my introduction could become another book, the beginning of the end...so to speak, so I will try to let the words in the poems speak for me. Perhaps you will grasp the essence on your souls as well, as you read the words God spoke to me – His heart He shared with me, in all my frailness and fragility. All those times we fail and cry, He sees: He knows them because He came to share them with us.

He shares so much really. I have recently seen He channels through His spirit waves – for instance: Charles Stanley recently spoke about spiritual gifts from God. He calls spirit, charisma – or divine grace freely given. Many of us feel powerless and weak often in life, not knowing or realizing we have much potential and that we are worthy sacred souls with much to offer. It is so heartfelt to see God show up in all the craziness, refine and quicken us, as He helps us overcome the multitude of defences that entrap us. We are meant to be whole – we are souls making our way to our true home. Feels like an eternity to me at times, but it is a light that beckons me, and one I hope will not grow too dim for me. I really want to keep trying to seek the source...I like the energy so far.

Reaching out a little, the efforts have been quite rewarding. He sharpens, refines and polishes the tarnished rough edges so that they will shine a bit stronger as I hobble on through, in hope that others may see that light too, pick up some of His energy to share for the common good, the greater good – for the Great God.

I'll close with some of my favourite words from God from Joel 2:25: "I will restore to you the years that the locust hat eaten, the canker worm, and the caterpillar, and the palmerworm, my great army which I Have sent among you." Yes, the Lord says He will make compensation to us, to bring everything back to us we have lost in the journey. He will bring the weary travellers home again and we will reclaim it all again. I am just so happy He has come to aid me in my journey, to make sure I get there intact. I thank Him for that, it's an awfully big load I know, but I rest along the way in His promises. I thank Him for all these words He gives in this book of His called the Holy Bible, and all the other words He ministers. I'm grabbing on greedily and happily.

No matter how long we've been down and out, dragged through the mud, or otherwise tossed about or cast aside, He gives us a hope and expectation for a great outcome. Jeremiah 29:11 tells us, "For I know the thoughts and plans that I think towards you, saith the Lord, thoughts of peace and not of evil, to give you hope and an expected end", and He adds, "Come unto me, all ye who that labour and are heavy-laden, and I will give you rest. Take my yoke upon you and learn of me; for I am meek and lowly in heart: and ye shall find rest unto your souls; For my yoke is easy and my burden is light." (Matthew 11:28)

So I now take my leave as I see His sun is smiling on me today, so off I go. I hear the birds calling now. I must go and tend to their welcoming calls...reflect some on what they too, have to say.

Ode To A Friend

Jesus's touch is so sweet,
    A
Songbird in the morn.
    Smile that glitters in my soul
So fresh, so soft,
    A loving delight.

Oh, sweet repose
    In embrace so near
Such love, such peace
    Why must I fear?

His eyes never leave me,
    Keep shining so bright.
They glitter and dance
    In the shadows of night.

Such merry cheer and bursts of delight
    Pour out in the morn
From my friend who holds tight.
    No. never lets go; or tires of the plight.

Just lifts on strong shoulders,
    Treading rock, sand, and clay
To His mountain of treasures
    We'll see on the way.

The Rock of Gibraltar
    Our burdens he'll take,
Scatter to wind, holy hills,
    And great lake.

Our Father in heaven,
    Precious Father so dear.
Hands so strong, voice so clear.

Beckons His loved ones:
    "I'm here; come near.
Come close by my side
    While I brush tears aside.
Let's sit by the water
    And watch the great tide.
I'll stay by your side and forever abide."

A Moment With Christ

Easy fluid, wisps of breeze
    Moments of love
Flow through with ease

Each fold of his garments,
    So white and bright
He's close now, near in sight.

Whispers words of enchantment to him who will hear
    The melodic refrain of his angels near

Singing songs of glory, delight, and cheer.
    Removing dark shadows and traces of fear.

Tis but a flash, this moment in time.
    Gently, softly touching – his great hand to mine.

Kind Sir, who am I to deserve this new bliss
    From sorrow and pain and plans gone amiss?

Oh, sweet child, think not I don't see
    Your sweet soul, your compassion, and great love for me.

You're one of my stars that twinkle and guide
    Our way back to heaven, passing through the divide.

So think not it strange I've come to your side
    To tarry awhile – bring back your sweet smile,
You know I really have missed for awhile.

Thank You, Jesus, for coming and sharing with me
    Your heart of pure gold and great majesty.

You've been a grand treasure I've kept stored away,
    Tucked in so tightly – borrowed from each day

Little pieces of heaven you have on display
    Samples from You we'll find in new ways.

Thanks for your patience, your love, and your signs,
    My friend and my anchor, oh, sweet, sweet divine.

Light in the Storm

God spoke to me through trials and throes,
    Through lashings and torments the enemy threw.
His aim to dash hope, but God only knows
    The seeds he'd been planting could surely renew;
Grow in great beauty and grace,
    Bringing lightness and dancing instead of disgrace.

Of oppression, against all of God's plans
    To prosper, to live, to feel lightness again.
Who is this creation who calls himself man
    Feels so entitled to bring others pain?

We get up in faith and begin a new day
    To be hated and mocked and knocked down again.

God says He has given us the right to be here,
    To take each new day He has given so free.

But the hate keeps on raging; no rest does it take
    To rattle, to batter, and make one's soul shake.
This dream that is happening, must surely awake
    To cherish a day that is lovely and safe.

No target is missed as they go after their prey.
    The innocents, their loved ones – they'll stomp on their way.
Their poisons are toxic; they spread them at will
    So freely, so widely to make their great kill.
No second thoughts given, only loving the thrill.
    Seek pain and destruction; no ponderance of they,
Just rid them of any who get in their way.

Round each corner and step, always there, lying wait,
    No lawful script have they to take -
The right to walk through their impenetrable gate;
    All done in such secrecy,
No regard for others or their privacy.

Their snares, their traps are set so tight -
    No chance of letting in the light;
Seems to be no friend in sight -
    To lessen the burdens on one soul's plight.

Albeit, we are like His cherished doves
    He loves, he treasures – takes such delight.
He'll lift those birds out of the fray,
    Get them up and on their way.

The scars and bruises left from the scourge
    Our wonderful healer will come and purge.
He'll heal us and lift us and bring us to dine -
    To a world of beauty of his true design.

Free Space

The daisies are fragrant
    Each time that I pass;
They wave and sway gently
    Beside the knoll's grass.

Their motion is easy,
    No struggle or toil --
Easy and breezy,
    Taking root in the soil.

They call me and bid me,
    Come join in the flow.
We'll feel the morn sun,
    And take things real slow.

Come! Up on your feet.
    Follow me to – the place of no care
To view only splendor,
    And never defeat.

The trees and the blossoms,
    All friends of mine,
Will be our kind hosts
    In this moment in time.

Keep trying to beckon me,
    Telling me we have-
So much to see.

Our Maker has given this day to connect,
    To cast aside worries,
Those things to reject.

Listen real closely
    In stillness of air.
Hear His calls of contentment
    He so wants to share.

The sights and the sounds-
    So near and so clear
Tip-toe in softly
    Like feet of the deer.

Look around, and inhale the scents of the day:
    The breath of the lily, the tulip and rose,
Caressing our senses,
    This freshness of May.

Calling Stars

My friends now in heaven waiting for me
    To show me the way
With smiles and bidding's of welcome and glee

Beguiling their presence, dear ones we've known well
    Seek sweet re connection, with stories to tell

Hearts and souls lying open, not blocked anymore,
    Not hidden or broken, just true to the core

Alive in the newness and eager to share
    New thoughts of refreshment – all feelings laid bare

Spirits of Grace, our ones of a kind,
    Bringing contentment and such peace of mind

These seeds that we planted many eons ago,
    Back now again with faces aglow.

Here now with their presence alive in this place
    With dancing, toes tapping, and smiles on their faces!

New trails discovered, paths found each day
    Will lead back together to map out the way.

The light that was blocked with shadows made dim
    Will shine once again to bring in our kin

Those stars we both looked at on many a night
    Are here now and shining so clear and so bright!

I've reached out and touched them, held close in my hand.
    I know you would really think it quite grand!

The sparkles and glitters of my floating heart,
    Reminders to you – we're not far apart.

My soldiers of this great galaxy, walk soft through the air
    Midst songs of love sweet and fair.
I'll wait for you in the valley so bright,
    Hold on real tight, with all of my might.

So, smile and know I am happy
    And so ...

Each day that comes round -
    Just jump on that old merry-go-round.
Take one of your horses of choice;
    Hear each piece of song and each pitch of voice.
Ride up and ride down as we fly through the air
    And see all the stars that still remain there.

No instruments needed for sight or for ear,
    Always so close to those we hold dear.
No fine-tuning adjustments or strings that will break
    Or other distractions this attachment can shake.

This magical mystery ride, this great rhapsody
    Casts out all intruders – no chance to divide
True souls of heaven called there to reside.

To Set Us Free

Such a young lad, made ready with kit bag in hand
    To fight a new fight in another strange land.
They said it was needed to cross the great sea
    In order to ensure we all could be free.

I tried to believe it all could be true.
    Hard for my mind to conceive -
I felt so alone… so sad and blue.

It was a big family I was leaving behind,
    But I who was chosen and I who must stand.
What did I know about marching and drills
    And enemies lurking behind all those hills?

With heart beating quickly and ammo in tow,
    Boots treading deeply through mud, sleet, and snow,
To dig new ditches – in hopes of restraining and keeping at bay-
    Those others we knew not but must keep away.

The faceless and nameless guy on that line,
    I'm told can never be no friend of mine.
I've known bad times, hurts, and great ills -
    But never did I really think I could kill.

I must carry on; - the mission is clear.
    You cannot let—the enemy near,
Or think of the things you once held so dear.
    Yet on brief ceasing of enemy fire,
I just go on thinking of things I desire.

I feel my fountain of youth slipping away,
    My firm resolution-tending to sway.
To hate and take orders, we are taught to obey --
    Surely not the kind of games I wanted to play.

There's a new gal back home who's waiting for me,
    I truly desire and soon hope to see.
We'll share some more laughter, a two-step and jig,
    Good music, good whiskey-I'll take my fair swig.
To these thoughts I turn to while I lie in wait;
    Can't think on no more; there's too much at stake.

Seems what I'm seeing too trying a task--
    Places I've been all wear the same mask.
Colors and shapes and smells of this war-
    Are really quite daunting,- I truly abhor.

That young man sent marching, so tall and free,
    In hopes of a future and a new family tree.
Got lost in the sights, now feels small – no longer can see.

The pictures, the memories; they come late at night:
    Those screams that pierced sharply, they gave us such fright.

Dear father, if only you'd shared,
    More of your story, your burdens we'd bear.
We'd lighten your shoulders and give you some rest
    From fear and resentment—all of those tests.

The light that shone brightly from big eyes so blue,
    Now faded and clouded by the smoke and the hue.
You kept them inside for all of those years,
    Just stemmed up the tide – no sign of your tears.
Those who walked beside you no longer will see.
    No hopes for a future or new gal for he.
The sorrow, the pain, the sad tragedy
    Of heroes we've lost – and still we're not free.

I try hard to fill that one special place-
    That lies empty without you;
And yearn to catch, one more glimpse of your face.

I think of you often in memory and such.
   Please know you are seen and loved very much.

We must keep the faith. Oh Lord hear our plea.
   You're kept safe in heaven, and again we will see.

Not So Small

I wonder what they've come to show,
    Those people who thought they were in the know.

They said that they would govern well -
    Serve our best interests, all worries quell.

This world continues to populate; yet why so hard to generate
    More trust and love, more equal stakes,
Not just for some but for all our sake?

I am real young, still having fun
    But at times I turn around to see,
People who don't seem to care -
    About all those trees over there,
That help us breathe, shade from the sun,
    Give gentle rest when day is done.

I know my parents too must care,
    But don't often have time to share.
I know they love us quite a lot,
    Guess they want us to worry not.
I think we are truly blessed,
    And that they really do their best.

So many things that bring delight,
    Why do others want to fight?

Sometimes I watch TV. at night,
    I see them call each other names
Look at each other with disdain -
    It seems it must cause them pain.

There's a world called democracy
    I hope it means we'll all agree,
To make new laws and new decrees.

To love your neighbor as yourself -
    It's what they teach us at our school.
Its really hard to understand it all,
    They so big – I so small.

Why can't we make each other free?
    Give the captives liberty,
From tyranny – make no man fool.
    Offer steps to climb above, not stuck below.
Reach out and help our dear fellow.

They seem so big and powerful;
    I did not think they could be so wrong.
I hope that they will tell the truth.
    They stand so sure, straight and tall -
Why do they let so many fall?

They'll feed the poor and heed their call,
    Help the many in despair.
Then everyone will have their share.

Let's rise above – not sink low,
    All because of that great ego.

I think we should sit down to talk-not mock,
    Of things like love and due respect.
None of these things we should neglect.

Make haste and step up to the plate,
    No longer stall or hesitate.

The world needs more with courage -
    Not to hinder, but encourage.
To seek a better world, give new hope,
    Get them off that sliding slope.

Now it's time to go to bed -
    Dream some dreams of whats ahead,
Thanksgiving time that's almost here
    Things to be thankful and of good cheer.
This soft pillow for my head, cuddled up in my bed.

I know its all in God's good grace -
    To be a part of the human race.
Many others have not such fun,
    I pray it can be undone.
If we all will lend our voice -
    Then everyone can have a choice.

I'm young and small, but one day will be tall.
    I hope that I will surely find, birds in the sky -
Lets heed the call for leaves on trees,
    Still giving shade and air to breathe.
These things I dream and hope I'll see.

Life Journey

I remember back for you and me,
    On those first days of pregnancy,
Kept you warm, close to my heart,
    Filled with love from the start.

Because I'd tried this road before,
    I felt no dread – just joy in store.

It was a time of festivity for Dad, your brother, and me.
    Looking back on those days, the memories I know will last.

We walked and played and had such fun,
    Your brother – he liked to run.
We danced and sang those happy songs,
    Sharon, Lois and Bram, in memory rang

Took nice walks through the snow
    Watched all the lights aglow.
Felt good and right to build our nest,
    Put our hearts and minds to rest.

I knew the time was close at hand, I was so big – could hardly stand.
    No new positions to sleep at night, not a single toe in sight.

And as those tugs increased their strength, through the night and morn -
    Knew our child would soon be born
Never thought it would go that fast, had thought the pains would last.

Time to hurry now and go, no time for worry or fuss.
    Just call up Dad and let him know, time to get back on that bus,
Turn back around and be with us.

Just one stop along the way, drop our son at school of play.
    Stay on the move – don't delay, pains were finally here to stay;
Though not too strong, were growing long.

In those final throes of pain, lightly stepped across those floors-
    Reach that desk, my only aim.
Even through the many stares, willed shaky legs – get me there.
    I did quite well, I did not choke, at least until my water broke.

They whisked me up that lift so fast, the pains were long and harder now,
    Though not much longer would they last -
Lost forever not a trace, just glad to see your lovely face.

Kept you close in my arms, tried to shelter you from harm.
    You were God's gift that day, and in his light you'll stay.
God's Xmas gift of glory, such a big part of the story.

From the time you first arrived, made such a difference in our lives.
    Your kind heart and easy ways,
Have cheered and lightened others days.
    You've always been a friend you know,
To those who've known you above, below.

I didn't always do things right, but in my thoughts I've held you tight.

The Chimes of Stillness

It doesn't seem so long from here to there -
    Said this soul one long and thoughtful night
Just time to spend…
    Minute… the toll.

This quiet space envelops me.
    No thoughts to disquiet… His Gift – it's free.

No big clock to click and wind,
    Break this ease within my mind.

It's luxury of Here and Now,
    To this only, I do now bow.

The morning light shall soon come round,
    And bring therein, it's own new sound.

I know the time will come again,
    For me to pause and give reflect-
To other places and events.
    But to this moment now, I give respect
This grace for me… is time well spent.

New Owner

Sign on the dotted line... my entrance to Heaven-
    In His honored time.
Endorse the new lease to this glorious throne

Sentence will be served concurrently,
    With Him in this new vicinity
The judgment... a lifetime, no chance to escape.
    This dwelling to be, my new found fate

Faced much opposition, ploughed many a road
    Ready for transition, shrug off the load

Scenes will be different after awhile
    No holes and thorns, to stumble and trip
Just easy footing – a sure solid grip

It appears they'll be no early release
    From tensions and turmoil – all of that strife
He says: just keep moving ahead;
    You know I am, The Way and The Life.

No walls or cells built to confine or place us in hell
    His walls are permeable – walk on straight through.
We'll all live together; in peace we will dwell.

Many a set back we've met on the way -
    Lost years and lost friendships, and so much dismay.
They're filed away in my library above,
    Chapters of memories – proofs of your love.

All bought and paid for – no further appeals.
    The wounds in my hands have made them all real.

This deed I hand you, titled – free and clear,
    Purchased by blood, to bring you again near.

You'll see friends and angels with favor and grace,
    Bringing smiles and warm handshakes, our new loving mates.
No guards standing there – with hate on their face.

The furnishings are uniquely designed,
    Molded for comfort – withstanding time.
The architect has taken great many pains
    In producing perfection, not leaving a stain.

His willing assistants have all lent a hand,
    Cleaned aired and dusted, made shiny and bright.
Opened grand windows to let in The Light.

Yesterday's struggles will live in the past;
    Friendly relations will be there to last.
It's been rather trying, I fully agree -
    But there's pleasure in knowing, you soon will be free.

Finishing touches are now put in place -
    Welcome mat at the door – hung curtains of lace.
You know it will well worth the wait -
    When you finally arrive, and open that gate!
Your initials are carved and crafted in stone,
    Gilded in love, silver and gold.

No chance to miss when making your way -
    This homecoming party done up with flair.
Heartening to see these people who care.

Their purpose is wanting to give you a home,
    To fully ensure, your no longer alone.

Night Beats

On awakening, still with Thee,
    With thoughts of rhyme and poetry.
Last nights storm bringing rain... oddly calming

Pouring down – beats in time, in sync with heart,
    Acrid thoughts residing there ...
Somehow rinsed and washed away

Strumming chords floating fair
    Resounding back to him in prayer

There is no tempest that resides
    Just songs of peace to clear the air

Speak to me – just lie in rest
    Renew my strength ... keep me blessed

Long Lost

Searching for identity
    Been a task of some degree

I've pondered some along the way
    Quite obscured, many a day

I've found it hard to co-exist -
    With others who claimed priority
You see there really was no time for me

The place I lived a revolving door
    Of rage and fury, fights galore
Erupting unexpectedly – late at night when fast asleep

Thought if I just closed my eyes
    I'd find a place where I could hide

I yearned for peace and space sometimes,
    To jog some memories in my mind,
Of happy times love and trust

Fleeting now, so long ago
    Not soon again will come to know

Wings on Air

God is light on his feet
    In dreams picks me up
        Moving with swirling light

Casts from eyes .. I see
        Makes me fly, no touch need be -
Encompasses Me.
    Glee … surrounding me

Here There Everywhere, Hearts Spinning Twirling
    Reaching out tenderly to join with me

Presence shared, moving souls, rightly paired
    Lifted Up on angels wings …
Rays of joy he brings

Embraced

In my dreams you came to me,
    Not up front among-st the throngs,
But in the back – still and strong

You always were a friend I know,
    Willingly gave, did bestow …
A family where I could belong,
    Giving hands to help me grow

So much a part of yesterday
    Yet still today…

The moments come suddenly,
    In my dreams—still there.
Really nice to know you care

Some feelings are hard to change
    Disregard, re-arrange

How I'd let things get away -
    Ponder on, still today

Though you left with some regret,
    Now in dreams will not forget

Your steady unassuming force,
    Can not easily be divorced

Smiling face I once knew cannot ever be erased
    Rests in my heart – keeps its place

Last night you came around again in my dreams
    There, wanting to be seen

Not only did I see your face; I had the luxury of your embrace
    Your hand that slid around my waist, felt so real again ...To feel
Comfort, that you gave to me

Thanks for stopping by again, spending time with me good friend
    Thought that was all part of the past,
Guess some things are meant to last

When it was time to go,
    I loosed my grip that linked with yours.
You kept your arm around my waist,
    Still holding on to that embrace

I didn't want to let you go
    This I'm sure you had to know.
You leaned over, bent your knee,
    Stood there strong and looked at me

So we were eye to eye -
    No differences or words to share;
Only just to linger there

You weren't the type of guy that could easily say good-bye
    ... Never really saw you cry

Even when you grew so weak -
    You fought that fight so valiantly.
Some things God builds are just too tough.
    You were a diamond in the rough.

Yes. Still our star up in the sky;
    Just so very plain to me -
Some things you bury just can't die.
    Presence permeating time,
No form or matter or lineage line

Taking on faces unique to us,
    Creations of love – From Above

Mountain Reflection

I see Thee in all Thy Majesty reaching eternally;
    There to greet me in the morn,
Echoes hopes to be reborn.

Breaking out among st the trees,
    Standing proud and looming free -
Takes the very breath of me

Stretched yourself in the air,
    Added beauty for all to share.

Oh great creator lost is he -
    Who looks on you but cannot see.

Granite peaks widely spaced,
    Endure forever in all grace.

Dimensions deep your stillness calls,
    Layered deep within your walls.

Looking out through pane and glass,
    Nothing else to block my view.

I see your future and your past,
    Giving space for full review.

Though mist and fog come to shroud;
    Will not easily cover thee -
With all your girth and chemistry,
    Even there among the clouds.

The hand of God has made it plain,
    Your hard to be invisible.
This is your land—of his domain.

The Word

Get up do those dishes stat!
    Then I'll have more time to pray

Important that I stay on track.
    This is how I'll start my day

Love and honor truth and song,
    Owed to him, to him belong

These are words he's given me
    Renews my strength – helps me pray

Vital things I shan't delay
    Sing them out – shout about!

Lightens things that look so bleak,
    Keeps me strong throughout my week

As I hold my Bible near – get down on my bended knee
    I know He'll loosen all the fears:
He died for me—he'll keep me free

He's called "The Word" - he speaks to me
    With songs of hope and liberty;
Trills in poems and rhyme and verse
    Floats in free – cannot rehearse

Keeps me safe from alarm, all the devils aims to harm
    So to give him my respect – for all the things he's given me -
My intentions sent to reflect, give him thanks – genuflect
    Make haste to do – wont neglect

Their Cross

Kept held down – made to look the clown;
    Couldn't take away your crown,
Or the glow upon your face;
    Couldn't help but stay in grace

They nailed you to that tree -
    Thinking that would set them free.
All that hate and blame – cast on you;
    To take away your holy name

The nails inflicted on that cross,
    Would very soon become their loss.
The truths they buried in their souls -
    Would shake shiver quake and roll.
Crying out to tell their story, boiling up – taking toll.
    Soon be sorry, all they wanted, was their glory

So much lost on that dark day; if only some had taken pause,
    Don't think any thought to pray,
Was this the right and proper way?

Taught to follow unjust laws, inflicting harm,– that wrongful right
    Only self did they befriend.
Guess they had no god but them.

I believe some were Christians in their right -
    Didn't seem to shed much light,
Murder, mayhem, fraught with strife.
    Taking our Dear Savior's life.

Where did they go then at end of day, to which god then, did they pray?
    To tell of how they had their fun -
That cannot easily be undone.

I felt the need to sit in prayer, with you share ...
    Don't think its right to take mans life in their hands -
Rip and twist and throw it away.

The Pilate said it was alright,
    To continue this ungodly fight -
Against this one solitary soul;
    What did they truly hope to gain?
Was it really worth all that pain?

No longer there with the throngs -
    To back them up, defend their stand,
Make them believe – they belonged,
    Inciting hatred throughout the land.

The time was coming, drawing near
    Soon they'd be alone at night;
A time of reckoning—maybe fear -
    Only soul could put aright.

I see Jesus struggling on that road, only slipping once or twice -
    Still carrying all that load.
What thanks we owe the awesome Christ!

We know its not the end of your story,
    You'll come again in unspeakable glory

After-Sounds

You are lyrics; you sing clear -
    Not just the music or the song;
Your the author – in the book.
    Spell it out intrinsically,
Not about religiosity.

Still to blame when things go wrong,
    Man, he carries his own ideas -
Slanted by the enemy.
    God's the one who keeps us free.

We're the dust sweeping through, by strong winds—breezes too
    Particles among-st the sand,
Settle in ... fall in line

Sequences of his unique design,
    Reflections of one true mind -
Never random pleasantries.

Still He's given all free choice:
    Love the song, yet hear the voice

Open Road

I see Your gate opening to me, creating space and liberty.
    Moving slowly, creaking wide,
Draws me through – it's divide.
    Care not much bout whats ahead,
    Feet just want to tread and tread.

Pure white snow all around -
    Falling down upon the ground.
Nothing to pollute the air,
    Only light and goodness there.

Dream-like trance it carries me,
    Easy motion step-by-step,
Floating free through gravity.

No sight or sound throughout this walk,
    To disturb me plague or stalk.

Just free movement mile by mile,
    Unending peace that makes me smile.

Rebound

You said you would never lie,
    Not forsake or leave too long
Be back soon – by and by.

You've given many words to me;
    Your life in rhyme – in poetry.
I'd like to give some back to you.
    In honor, thanks, please do review.

No parallel, no measure
    You just indwell -
You are my treasure.

Jehovah – Shammah, one name of many;
    It means, "The Lord is There"
I sure feel You in the air.

I'll lean on you right to the end,
    On you, for sure I can depend.

There is much to say ...
    I'll save it for another day
Suspect you'll have more to share,
    You truly are a God who cares!

Today you've come on really strong;
    It really seems to ring so true,
Gifts from you—to you belong.

Thanks for stepping out this way -
    You came and took my breath away.
Such a lovely state of grace,
    Ensured our meeting – face to face.

Sights and Sounds

I remember when I saw your face,
    Blue eyes peering up at me.
The first time you opened your eyes,
    Giving heart such a thrill.

Nestled in my arms, safe and sound from all alarm.
    Found your way into my heart.

After-shock from earthquake near -
    Felt it rock and sway the room.
Will not soon, forget that boom.

His gifts of love and grace that day -
    Resounding in His special ways:

Strength and might, softness and light
    Parallel worlds—Miracles

Touched

Oh Sweet God I hear Your Voice
    Just a few words – they help me rejoice

Mighty Books – Impaled in me ... generously
    Struck my heart

Thought you'd gone and left me be;
    But see your face – to the ninth degree,
Not just in the near local, but sitting here in front of me.

Heard some words in which you spoke,
    Seemed to poke, stroke, invoke;
Live in me, diametrically.

I know Your words have power true -
    The Bible tells it openly.
Their beauty seems to lift the blues.

One touch from your mighty hand,
    Brings the sun to light my land.

You really are such fun you know,
    Within this dance, you help faith grow.

I've found you also like to play -
    Amazing way to start my day!
So many treats you've showed today.

This isn't a side I've seen awhile,
    You've come to me—bringing both a smile.

I'd thought you'd gone, but cannot be;
    So kind to bring my loves to me!
To see their faces, feel their touch.

Their good and well, happy, sound.
    Thank you God so very much!

The Prayer

Dear Papa not sure about your plan;
    If I need to take a stand -
Or think about on this new day,
    But, I know, I need to pray.

Times I'm lost and do not know -
    Proper way I need to go.

My greatest friend I have in thee.
    Please stay with me and help me grow;
Keep me strong, instill in me;
    Your Will, keep in stow – help me see.

Words can't seem to speak about, please enlighten them today.
    Here – I'll write them in plain view:
Keep all your saints close to you.

Dear Jesus come, don't pass them by,
    They need you now – I cannot lie
Your life, your ove, your lullabies.
    Refresh them as your morning dew!

No longer have them here with me -
    Can't rock them them back to sleep.
Have to give them back to you – in grace please keep.
    Ease their cares, stroke their hair.

Reaching out with hands still pierced,
    Please extend with open arms, eternal love for us so fierce.
Keep them safe, from all harm.

On The Inside

Bring Your Might, Oh God, bring it strong!
    By the Father – through the Son.
Holy Spirit – live in me.

Fluid luminosity passing through,
    Astral channels, eclipsing soul -
Tingling skin, metaphysical light.

Sways and swirls… turns and toils,
    Cupping chords, circles joy, entwine-en coil,
Runs through my veins, straight to my heart.

Brought together cohesively, easy touching, lightly through,
    Stirring love in chambers bare, tentacles reaching everywhere,
Circulating, each cell renews, gives us life, again, anew

Communion

I see Your Light Jesus, I feel it with me,
    Your right there beside me calling me in . .

Can't think of mere words to describe,
    Yet surely a feeling I'm feeling within.

How is it your here so often with me,
    To soften and loosen all debris?
Smoothing out edges from all surface cares-
    Bringing omnipotent presence to share.

Heart Strings

Love takes but a moment in eternity time,
    Stops for awhile; makes heart smile

So many moments from long ago,
    Flashes in time of people you know

But nothing to compare or contrast
    Than those of a child – they always will last

So many to choose, which shall I pick?
    Here's one I will share, I know it will stick

Those times were fleeting and long ago,
    When you were little – watching you grow

So much time – open and free,
    Seemed in that moment . . was just you and me

Was not the games or rides that day
    Calling you to come and play,
But puppets dancing, that brought you their way

Entranced with their magic your face affixed,
    You watched in amazement—Surely a trick?

Their graceful lilting and bowing
    To strings were attached; just seemed to fly!
Bringing pure wonder from bright shiny eyes

I think there's no better a sight I have seen
    Then seeing a wee child so happy and free,
My son there beside me, filled with glee

Where did they come from – where did they go,
   All of those puppets that moved to and fro?
Tugging our hearts, drawing us in..

Please listen . . I want you to know
   You were the main part – the star of the show,
And just like that star . . every brightly you glow

Birds in Flight

I believe they have their doubts in you
    May be a God of disrepair
Please show up – let them know you care

Meet their needs,
    Doors that closed – bring lights of hope
Plant some tiny mustard seeds

Help to cope, lift them up,
    Feed the broken damaged reeds
.. Bind their wounds

Perhaps a farthing or a shilling
    Not much cost to bridge the gap – draw in close
.. Seek the lost

Like the swallows, restless all
    Crying out, calling You
Hear them now—restore, renew

Moving On

It's not from the beauty that's part of this land,
    His gifts in Creation – from his loving hand.

It's just the disruptions – from them I do flee,
    Find new places and people to see.

With hope in my heart and prayers in my mind,
    Make a new start, hidden treasures to find.

Perhaps lying dormant in places somewhere,
    Are hearts full of peace in people who care.
I know from my loved ones I'm still far apart -
    But never can be too far from my heart.
Think I'll just try to make a new start.

Mixed feelings live here of journey so near,
    But like others I've had, I'll try not to fear;
Just keep moving, find open road;
    Though not alone I'll be when I roam -
He'll still be with me to carry the load,
    Till He says, "Enough", and brings me on home.

Strength of Heart

Unveil Yourself, break the barrier, slit the seal, Your will reveal,
      Bring to Light – Come – Begin

Befriend – shine bright—so near in sight;
      Blinded eyes, to thee look.
Hearts that slope, broken sides, patch them up, last awhile.

In the middle – still beats strong -
      Only skips a beat or two.

Harsh-flung words, made some blue
      Though rugged made – can't easily invade

Love From you, knows the face
      His handwork – keeps the pace, stays in stride

He lives there – watches too, seeking all the broken parts
      Worn right out, fall – in time

Keep in mind their only leased, knows them well
      Designs – Parts of his master plan

That Time of Year

Christmas time dawning, soon again here
    Yet something's amiss – no, not quite alright
Where did the year go, sped by so fast,
    Was always here, now part of past

Moments in time, - stopped in their tracks
    The day he left, took reprieve
So many Christmas's – was just you and he
    I know you will think on, and sometimes grieve

I'd like to try and bring some cheer -
    Always in my heart and thoughts
Not much else to say or do -
    Some things will simply make you blue

Still be brighter days ahead, may good things yet in store
    Where other gifts and treasures live -
In a different time, a different place

Kind of like Christmas but new roust-a bouts
    May not be tinsel, holly or snow…
But plenty of magical glory I'm told
    No Rudolph the Reindeer guiding the sleigh
But chariots of gold, leading the way

All revived – calm and bright
    Triumphant glory – stringing harps
Cherubic faces filled with delight

I know your sure to meet again,
    Share some laughs and have some fun
So here's to you in this New Year,
    Please be well and happy son!

Aglow

Words strike like fire, light our hearts, warm our souls,
    Burn through all our woes and cares,
Consumes them up, turns to ash.

Crackles in the cool night air, igniting sparks, fan and flare -
    Gives light to brighten or cinders to burn,
Torches that scar and sear our hearts.

To help or wound, to heal or scorch,
    Let's cut through the haze -
Salve or balm, cure, or harm?

While sitting by the fireside chair,
    Think on thoughts and words to share,
Lift them up to God in prayer.

Let them kindle in your mind -
    Stir them round from time to time,
Stroke them, poke them, with faith aflame,
    Watch them burst and glow and shine.

Loving words like breath they blow,
    Mighty forces spread throughout -
Remove the shadows – gives light glow.

Washed and Renewed

Jehovah Jireh do rain down,
    All Your precious bliss befall.

So many names for You, all are precious – all renew.
    Each one I test and sometimes call,
Give thanks and honor, due respect;
    You fought and conquered sin and death.

Some tears still fall, can't quite dry – they've left their crease.
    Wish you'd come replace with peace.

You've paid my debts and shed your blood;
    Perhaps could offer, one more flood?
Bring some rain to wash away,
    All the thoughts of egos pains.

Your waves of inner sanctity will rinse all doubts from me.
    Renew me to increase my faith, make it true as sea is blue.

Sacred Sunday

In all my yesterdays, Sundays much too long a day,
> Stretching endlessly, confining me – never felt free.

Forced to go to church and pray,
> Kneel right down and bow my head;

Couldn't find a God who led,
> Just a priest who talked and talked -

Nothing that could interest me.
> Why was there no God who walked?

Only thing that kept me there, - of which I cared,
> Were the statues of the cross,

And Jesus suffering all that loss.

It was His pain that spoke to me;
> Pinned me down – held me there.

His love for me, tears for me—set me free.

Traveled years and miles since then lessons learned – lots of pain,
> Some remain, more to gain.

Though must have been some time well spent – even Lent.
> I've come to know him – see his smile ...

All those Sundays from before, no longer now, such a bore.

Now lots of time in the world to see sacredness
> Sacredness – blessedness,

Here in his presence face to face,
> He sits with me – gives me grace.

Unstuck

Come and stay with us today, give us grace – with love embrace
    Live in us, fill our hearts, lift us up
From the furrow and the fog – blot it out

God I need to move today, untangle knots from yesterday
    Bend and stretch, work it out… find a way

Help me walk like Jesus did, easy strides to keep his pace
    Smooth and slow and in his grace

Loose the stance that keeps me fixed
    Help me be more flexible

Unending curves and life's cruel twists
    Keep me in it's vice-like grip

New roads now been paved for me,
    Give me space unfettered – free

Mold me like plasticine, give new strength and breath to me
    Finish this race – eventually

Almost There

Pick up some pieces along the way,
    Try not to look too far behind
They'll still be there, they like to cling
    Thoughts of yore and yesterday,
All the old in memory bring -
    Many good, though some unkind

Raise my hand to clutch -
    That girl . . She's young, taking in some sun
Laughing – having fun, shared with light and airy friends
    Not many worries do attend

If I could simply just reach out, gather all, pieces of heart
    Pick them up, one by one, put them back, right in place
Where they belong – in yesterday

Now I must look away, no need to stay too long – in yesterday
    Just move along in this old world,
To my today, and my tomorrow;
    In time, may borrow – other joys - other sorrows

Their just a part of who I am,
    Spokes made up to fill one big whole
Of one deep soul

Encompass Us

Come bright, star shine on us – show your gleaming face
    … Encompass us

Make me stronger to share your burdens, bless and encourage
    Like You do: carry that cross

I just want to talk about you, care about you
    Love you too …

Be my guest, to you profess
    Take away my earthly cares, your being share

Armies of evil, set them down, find Your crown
    Encompassed in your mighty arms … not weighed down

In everything you say and do, help me grow
    … More like you

Petitions of Grace

Mighty land of provision, find that niche
    Extend it with your heart of gold -
Nuggets in Your Mighty Hand

Grant with light, shine it through, let it rest: just be,
    One of your miracles – see through it all

Some will be true, hear your call, encircle – fly sweet and low
    Beset – please bless

Distant Dreams

Dear Papa

Good morning – not feeling so well, still have some troubles,
    Please let me near
Thoughts of long ago, come in my sleep, can't put away

People I know, places I went, suited me then, now don't quite fit.
    OK. through the night, not the day
Wish I could take and turn them around,
    More love to be found – reality bound

Hard to live in two different worlds -
    Sometimes at night I take them and switch
Streamline in my mind – play or rewind

Wish I could do that at day – travel in time,
    Find people afar I love so,
Be here in time and watch them grow, again get to know.
    But just like my dreams – can't make them real,
Hurts too much to feel.

Wish I could be part of their day, sit with and play
    What a loving symbiosis it could be - were I to be free

Now for the hours that drift in the day – evolve into night,
    I'll highlight and play some … and dream them away

This Time

Thank You God for being there
    And that You care

Just set my stuff down right here
    Find a bit of gentle space …
Breathing in the scent of You

So quiet now, still and calm,
    Mind has stopped, not a peep
Breath is deep – no restlessness,
    … Not a single solitary sound

Valves of earth – all its waves,
    Now shut off somewhere afar
Only just… Holy air

Happens close around this time,
    You draw near
Not really sure who you're with
    Can't quite make it out

Loving tugs, settles – lifts
    Placid, sits so comfortable, lulls and soothes
Gentle drifting brings much peace – kind relief, sacred-pure
    Basking in a touch so fine, at this blessed Christmas time

Christmas Ties

Something very real – at Christmas time
    Touched and revealed by You

Even now, in the music – songs I hear
    Speak to me, differently

Can't get too far from you
    Books I read, dreams I dream

Currents make me want to sway
    Move a bit more close to you

Instrumentally you play, give me feet to rise above
    Fall in love all over again

The chords it strikes seem to bring much unity
    Closes gaps - mysteries – his hands unwrap

Treasured loves become unearthed -
    Can almost feel the angels there,
Proclaiming life birthed on that day

Breaking forth - join together new and old -
    Ribbons tied intrinsically, declare his love eternally,
Wrapped in songs we sing about

Rising Time

Don't lie in bed this morning
    And feel the enemy's attacks on you,
Already trying to shake you up and ruin your day,
    He's well-equipped to make you blue,
He doesn't like to see you pray.

Just wants to get his hands on you;
    Planned it for a long long time -
Funneled, crafted evil spells;
    Knows what dwells within your mind.

Don't let him change your heart – rise and shine in Jesus time!
    God's words of truth – do impart.
Throw them back, speak them out,
    Stay with Jesus – don't depart!

Put In Place

Can't stop Your mighty words flowing in to me today;
    Wasn't going to take this time to pray.

Each time I go about my day, God just seems to call me back,
    Placing tugs – here and there, throwing words out in the air.

No rhyme or reason -
    I think its part of the wonderful season.

Can't think of any other reason,
    I believe it gives him extra reason.

Instills His beauty, eases cares -
    Must thank him for his magnitude, his person-hood,
For all the help he gives to me, I profess to him my loyalty.

Consider Us

No one there tending your heart,
    Minding, listening, presiding with you,
Honoring you, reaching to you

Where are the mentors for young men today?
    You have to be strong, you're a man they say.
Why not reach out and give them a hand?

Don't look at the strength in muscle alone
    There's also the blood that runs through the bones

Been new strides made on the way,
    Protection of children, women's rights too
All wise intentions, its good, its OK.,
    Yet need a new movement – perspective and view

They want to be strong, to serve and protect,
    Been taught is their duty, in spite of their fears
Need some encouragement, been missed through the years

We need to be present, attune to them now
    To give them some time -
Listen to hearts, as well as to minds.

Let's give them some freedom and space,
    To feel all the feelings they've buried inside
Bring out in the open, more able to face

These young men are growing to be our men of today
    They need our attention, more mentors – good men,
More Dad's who will teach them and show them the way
    Makes such a difference, the roles that they play

Reach out and share, lighten their loads,
    Give them your knowledge – help them get there

Not trying to be better than you,
    Be proud if they want to be – just more like you.

Don't leave them too long to find their own path,
    Without any guidance their courage won't last

Turn now, let's meet it head-on
    Get rid of the rigid, restrictions of past
Castes put in place -
    We're all intricate special parts of this human race,
All part and parcel of one larger soul

Let's nourish their growth, identity too
    Make them feel they belong, help them be strong

Will make for a happier healthier world,
    Not much difference, be it boy or girl

All so unique, let's not stereotype
    God knows all our names – he sees every face
Don't set us apart – be kind and unite

Don't let jealousy anger or hate -
    Step into confuse us, or cause us to wait
Just settle the score by doing what's right

Hold My Hand

Don't think I've often mentioned
    Nor often talked about
Yet still of some convention
    Simple pleasures of the hand

That little girl walking by today
    Looked so happy with her Dad
Laughing skipping merrily, singing sweetly, bold and free
    Still so young and innocent -
Gently reaching for his hand

Seems a small and simple thing
    Yet so much exchanged therein;
It's a gift, the trust it brings

Reminding me of yesterday
    When I was like that little girl
My father took me by the hand
    Felt such warmth and strength within

Like when he'd lift and carry me
    Safe and strong within his arms
Made me feel 10 feet tall

Or when He'd throw me in the air -
    Never worried I would fall

Hold on to that embrace, They watch all the things you do
    They've got their eyes fixed on you – Look up to you

Seems like only yesterday
    Looked at you, born so new
Watched those tiny precious hands
    ..Clutched in mine

Don't ever think it's no big thing -
    The stories that those hands can tell
It really is a touching thing

In Search of Joy

Why is joy so hard to find
    Not many smiles in faces I see
Perchance may be, reflection in me?

Even in places of beauty and light
    Don't see much life in their eyes
No peels of laughter or bounce in their step
    Not even in children, I'd hoped to expect

Seems to be quite arduous a task
    Uncovering the answers to such questions I ask
Why so is joy so elusive in time?

Once long ago was easy to find
    Wish we could retrieve it again in this world
Why is it buried so wide and so deep?
    Along with compassion – they've both gone to sleep

Rather alarming as I sit and reflect
    These are all gifts of great magnitude
Given with love from God up above
    Better than toys and money and stuff -
I'm sure of these we've more than enough

Our deepest emotions that make us alive
    Again need to touch, to seek for and strive
Feel and touch, unlock and free

No longer robots, stiff and sad -
    Find goodness and truth deep in our souls
Make us be glad, happy and whole

Of The Sea

Blow in light and fair swept winds,
    Will not fell, but heal and bless
Unhook the cares of worldly strains,
    Only you can cast them out

Release from tempests tossed about – pressed in tight
    Midst the throes of earthly foes, steady us with hands of love
Oh Sweet Man from Galilee, can you see us churning round
    Ravaged from these stormy seas

Treading wildly, so alarmed, out too far – in too deep
    Slowly sinking – already in above our head
Chilled to bone and fraught with fear

I look to You, so often do -
    To calm the waters that swept through

Be an anchor for our souls,
    Too often seems to come unhinged

Stay – fold the waves; calm the hurling rushing sea
    Keep us safe in this flood, stable in your eyes- like doves
Help your loved ones rise above

Will only take a few small steps, part the waves – fetch us out
    Beaten weary-winded souls, steady us – set us free

Sun- drench us dry by the river bed
    Warm us up, feed our hearts
With peace be led – never be your castaways

Born To Reside

Our King and Heir is here
    Wants to refresh us and give us joy

Ease the pain – new footing to gain
    Reign in and wash out – all worry and doubt

As certain night will turn to day
    It's clear He's been born to come and stay

He came here at birth, unfolded his presence -
    Then gave us his word

It's higher and stronger than all human form
    Reaching new heights
Feeling the grace of our Lord Jesus Christ

Springs To Life

The soul recognizes poetry and music,
    From the depths from whence it came

Reaches in stillness,
    Touches with arms of love

Pours and shares sweet melodies,
    Enchains the heart, floods the soul
Calls us out eternally through cords of life – beats of time

Can only be the masters voice speaking through
    Wants to bring his pure white joy

Rejoice with us, romance and woo -
    Profound and simple chemistry

Elixing love molecules – mixes, fills
    Never find cacophony

Sweet and good – heartbeats in you
    Lulls the mind, soothes in kind

Lilting peace, touches – binds
    Feel the part, chant the notes
He's the thread that holds us there

Formless

To what pleasure do I owe this call
    A random visit; what tempest brews?

Don't think I recognize the form
    Can't see them in his family tree

Peculiar dimensions elongate
    Irregular, not soft, – their thick
Sitting solid, much like bricks

Seems the roots are too complex
    Oddly fixed – secular
Twisted deep can't be stirred
    They're fast asleep

The Claws of The Lion

With torture and torment they strike – blow after blow
    Not intermittent: repeatedly
This constant harassment, they know full well
    .. Is killing me

I know God will soon reform,
    He's offered restitution, absolution for me
Divinity, equality – in his eyes I see

I've lagged and staggered, been torn apart,
    Pierced the edges of my rugged heart -
Not been easy – left feeling forlorn

They've arched their backs, ready and poised;
    They're stalking their prey, God hear me pray.
Please give me courage to keep the pace,
    Provide constitution – develop my faith-
Ravage my soul, instead with your grace

Letting Go

The grace of my Father has given me,
    A new understanding – I must set them free

He says His plans are much greater than mine;
    To rest in his comfort and trust in his love

He has it in control, he's working it out,
    To Him I should look to – to him I should flee

Put away thoughts of worry within;
    He'll handle the world and all of it's sins

Much like the eagle, he fought it alone,
    Soared new heights in strength and power

If look too high may tend to sway -
    Don't look to clouds to come your way

Look for pleasant imagery,
    Step out in faith—he'll keep you safe

Don't think too much of what's ahead -
    Or be like Lot, and look back
.. Instead, just look to God.

Free to share His angel's wings -
    Keep you soaring above it all;
Be right there – to break your fall

It's OK To Cry

I feel such harassment, disturbance of mind
    Some people don't care if you're innocent or ill
Or who may be dying, at this holy time

Nothing is sacred, nothing at all
    In horror, God must be weeping - devil laughing with glee
Angels pause their singing—are down on their knees

Attacks from the enemy not given respite,
    Evil and hatred are really still quite rife
No matter the season – no compassion, respect, or value for life

Perhaps it will take a flood or a shake,
    To move them from such a neutral a state
Never has been such an urgent a cause -
    So filled with indifference, injustice and hate
Try to change it before it's too late

I'm told people cry when they know not what to do,
    No other expressions in sight or in view
Some things can't be touched with words or with voice
    Let the tears rain down, what else can they do?

Take time to reach out, share one tear or two,
    Hold onto the hand of one who is blue
They need some care, to tend to their wounds

God bless those who are able to cry
    Re-fill with your love, re-stock their supply -
Relieve sorrows pain

Stop others intentions to harm – speak out with your voice,
    Hold back their arms that reach out to maim -
It has to be quick, while they still have a choice

Your Host

God has spoken; taken aside, confided and given to me -
    More words that I need to know and to grow
Said, "Child hear my chide."

It's evening time, sunset is near;
    Important to listen, lean in very close.
Don't speak too loudly, proudly or boast -
    Be like Caspar, a nice friendly ghost

Just be my shadow – some light in the darkness,
    They won't have to grope
I'll be there beside you, to pass this new test;
    Speak words – to encourage and bless

I'm trying to come and live in you,
    Give some reflection for you to see through

You need to adhere, the end is quite near -
    Time to put old things away;
You need to believe I'm right there with you.
    I have much to offer – I'll give you some bread,
A taste to appease you, there's much more ahead.

Try to guide as we move through the day...
    Making our way -
Heavy in step, in my path be ye led

Just inch a bit closer, be my kind host;
    Both weary travelers in search of the sun,
Not too much further, in victory be one.

The Devil's Tails

They come courting fury, evil and rage – everything else is a facade.
    They're signaled to intimidate, infiltrate and invade -
Thinking they wear such a clever disguise,
    Can see its the devil over there on their side.

He's riding shotgun, hard to dispel,
    He's already claimed – condemned souls to hell

They've chosen this road, in him they believe
    They'll come to know soon – he means to deceive

Must be a hidden talent in them,
    His badge of honor – laid claim in his name -
Genetic his scheme, murder – mayhem

Likely was nurtured in seeds he'd sown;
    Long ago planted, in hopes they would grow,
Much like him in kind and form.

Live in his shadows wherever they go;
    Hard to conceive he'd be such a clutch -
Believe him so much, and even more surprising,
    How they would – enjoy it so much!

This ride is not meant for us all:
    Only to those who beckon his calls.
It ends in disaster and other pitfalls

No freedom or laughter or faces of glee,
    Only adapted for pure misery
No sing-a-longs—only hatred I see;
    All frozen in hell with the enemy

Elemental in Nature

They all have different voices, much like humans do
    Pitches and sounds, volumes and tones
Go up and down, making all sorts of sounds
    Add many a color to brighten your day

They come from all over the world -
    Some use some language, don't make a sound
Sometimes it's easy to understand, people say,
    By reading their lips, hearing them pray

Look for their meaning in the way that they play
    If their happy or sad in things that they say
Or love in their eyes – at times there are tears
    All creatures of God to share in this world,
He gives to all, be man, boy or girl

Listen and watch the birds of the air -
    Their calling out to some of their mates
Sing "cock-a-doodle-do – good morning to you"
    Perhaps they are love birds – making a date

The wrens are saying, "Come help me, I'm building a nest,
    For all of my young ones to lie here and rest"
The warbling of throat has just the right note – they'll understand

Or the hens calling young ones, garbling to them
    "Cluck cluck – move along"

Humming birds humming, their colors so bright,
    Blue birds are singing, welcoming spring

The dove is cooing—looking straight at you
    Owl watches too – sees what you do
His big shiny eyes, don't miss a beat

Busy bees hum when they work
    Stop to greet flowers – have a smell, take a look

Sometimes I wish we were more like the birds
    When we're afraid, know not what to do
Then we could just get up, fly away

But instead I call to God—he's my friend
    He helps me to think about other nice things
It's goodness he brings

I write the words down – sometimes I sing -
    About people I love, I thank him and say,
"Thank you Dear God for all that you bring" -
    So I can sit here and share some today

Poetically Just

Many thoughts and ideas abrew,
    Channeled, directed – coming from You.
Streamlined collections, old and new,
    Myriads of memories I now share with you.

Not about fame or laying claim;
    Only just that God's – been speaking your name.

Never dreamed I'd have the inclination or time,
    To formulate words and get them to rhyme,
Or bring them alive in stories to tell.

Of loved ones and dear ones, parts of our past;
    They're bound in our hearts and live on Page 2 -
The years have been fleeting – new ones in view

Not with a camera these pictures I give,
    But with pen and paper—in words that they live.
They spring from chambers, shutters and sights,
    Reflections of you now brought to life.

Don't want to erase them, let them fade too fast;
    Imprint them now – ensure they last.
Reached by the source – touched by the divine.

I trust poetic justice will give you your due -
    In things that you did, words that you said.
Reflections and angles and views,
    Will pause and rest right here in our head.

Good as Gold

Really quite simple, not a hard sell
    Something to cling to, not to repel

He's given something tangible,- all else slips away
    Quality untarnished; it's brilliant and bright

Word is like gold, can feel – it's concrete
    Vision unblemished, by heat or by light

Go ahead, chip away -
    The harder you pound it, the more solid it stays

Like hearts of compassion, refined by the grind,
    This rock is girded to last for all time
Lives up to it's words and stays just good as gold

Selah

Selah means pause and reflect;
    It's a new one for me, must say I respect

Inspired by words we spoke yesterday,
    Set them aside to come back to today

Try to find words I've come to forget,
    Went fishing for them, at the end of the line
Strung them together, hooked onto some
    Pictures of you I'd like to relay:

You're walking up the hill alone in the night,
    Seen only in shadows cast by city lights

Must have found some comfort in that night air,
    With fresh falling snow accompanying you there

Between the soul and treading of feet,
    Imagining peace surrounding that space

In softness and stillness moving quietly along
    Healing for heart, new ground to be reached

He has you in sight as you go on your way -
    May give you a song or perhaps clear your path
A word or a thought to keep you on track

There in the darkness he's waiting on top,
    To share in a smile or simply a touch
Shed some more light to make your way back,
    Just stand by your side or fly away with you

The Published Soul

Reunion, connections – a sorting of sorts
    Division of spirits, hearts to unite
The good that we did, souls that we failed

Given some time before the year ends
    Respect and attend – fences to mend

The lost child needed somewhere to belong -
    Must have been feeling forlorn and blue
Where else could you go, a lone little boy?

No tree-house to climb, confide troubles to,
    Only four walls to keep you within; to my chagrin,
There were other things—calling you in.
    A world of enticements, ploys and sins,
To rob you of your innocence.

Generous and kind, such love to give -
    Happy heart, laughter free;
Such a pleasant joyful guy

Hold onto your children, they won't be here long
    Find that needed space in heart
Hear it, let it be a part, that speaks to you of quality

Seek the beauty deep within,
    Share it now with those you love
Let it out – open up, not too late to rise above
    Layered there in the soul
Folds of humanity – help us heal,
    Make us whole

Curtan Calls

It's really just a conglomeration of things -
    That pull at your heart strings and cause them to sing.

To sweeten life's sorrows and bring hidden joys -
    Laughter to borrow therein;
Softening edges of life's bitter things.

I like to believe we're all young at heart,
    Looking at life through the eyes of a child,
Finding contentment in the simplest of things.

Like the pied piper they call out to you -
    With eyes of enchantment they filter it through,
Holding the spell with laughter and glee.

Spirits contagious through glistening eyes,
    Looking to you with love and with pride.

Put all else away, come to their theater -
    Watch their story of play.

Joyful Boy

Didn't much like to sleep—good thing you were so sweet!
    Even as a babe in womb, always active on the move.
Tumble turn, move and groove – keeping time to your own beat -
    Musical dancing baby feet.

Cool little guy – big bright smile and shiny eyes,
    Always ready to surprise, explore and run -
Sunshine on a cloudy day.

In nursery school too, the circle formed -
    Led the way in schools of play,
Life to the party, social, kind.

Before your brother was born, went to West Edmonton Mall.
    - Had lots of extra time to spare; you played and frolicked in the balls -
Diving, dashing in and out; peels of laughter ringing out.

Didn't understand when people cried, or why others could be mean.
    I tried to explain, said "sorry", he merely said, "Just don't do it" ..
End of story.

Simple times, so innocent and bright – only wanted just to play -
    Didn't matter the time – count on him to make your day.

Even young he was quite wise -
    In times of stress I'd get up to leave,
His little voice said, "Mommy, you beh-a-not leave"

Always trying to articulate; seemed quite coherent – clear to me -
    Hearts are hard to separate.

Now that boys become a man, still finds time in which to fly,
    Jumping fee when he sky-dives.

Glad we had that time to spend,
    Try and keep that joy, precious golden little boy.

Unflappable

Lets smooth things out, clear some air; loosen up, lighten care,
    Drop your jaw, let tension drain, perhaps neglect all worldly strain.

Lose the cause, lie on the couch—just because.
    Let things go – settle, rest, think of kinder sweeter things,
Remember back to pleasantries – nice connections keep us blessed.
    Though just in memories, they're welcome guests.

I like to think of special times - love within a family.
    Let me share a few… so long ago, before they grew:

Like baking just for fun; rolling dough, forming shapes -
    Gobs of stuff all over the place!

Even though you couldn't speak a lot, words only I could understand,
    We shared a language quite unique.
In your carriage taking walks, I'd hum and softly speak to you.
    You answered back, as if you knew;
There would be times I'd worry for you.

Small in that little bed, the nurses tried to keep you fed.
    They said you wouldn't talk to them, only reason when I'd attend.

Jumping up when it would snow, peering out that window pane -
    Saying, "Mommy, it's "noing out."

Sitting watching peacefully, swans float by – tranquilly.
    Caught up in that happy place, living life happily.

Both so busy growing up, captured in their energy.
    Water-slides, coaster rides, playing hockey in the street -
Roller-blades on their feet, or quietly sitting side by side - my quiet guy.
    Just happy sitting there – a sharing time, no need to move.
These are times that speak to me, times in life of sacredness.

Unload the shoulders; find a gentle flowing brook,
    Release the weights, set them down—free to float.
Nice to think on – bound in rhyme; kinder gentler thoughts to mind.

The Vibration of Christ

Reach out a little, He'll find a way to grab onto you
    He'll pull you back—stop the enemy in his tracks
Strip him with the words you say

Give some peace, please send its grip in waves of ease
    Solid, hardy, step in front; cut the core with power and might
Step on up, stand and fight

Send Your angels, all their friends – we'll know they're saints you sent
    Able, ready—seize the day!

Touch them in their heavy spots, hold within a soul that's blue
    Give new hearts – starts of joy
Set us in your heavenly sights, plug us in – power us through

Fasten to your chords of light, connect with us – umbilically
    Place your hands around our souls. inoculate us—make us whole

Afflicted

Waves of affliction jump heavy on my back
    Daggers thrown – sucker punched
Knocks the wind right out of me; takes me to the floor

You heard and felt and saw them all, took the weight and carried through
    Inched Your way along the ground—stood back up, climbed out again
Each time you fell you rose above

See You suffer for my shame, so awfully far from even ground
    You did it all to clear my name

Let me try to compensate, fall down at your feet and weep
    Pray I can be more like you – follow you
Help you on that rugged path, share that cross – walk there too

For The Good Times

Hey Dad,

I'm remembering you,

Been a long time, old pal of mine!
    Got you here, pen and paper near
I think it's the right time to sit and talk,
    Drop you a note, long overdue—don't you think?

Didn't talk much back then, though I think you tried
    Think we had some trouble in our childhoods -
Never quite knew where we stood

Wanted to wait till this time of year;
    Was always the time we tried to draw near
Dad, you'd always bring the tree, one of your jobs - You busy guy!
    Chief cook and bottle washer tending the bar
I'm convinced you deserved and rated more stripes and stars!

I hear Perry Como at just the right times,
    Precisely the times as you come to mind!
Always a purpose with him don't you know?
    Much like the magic of fresh falling snow

I hear him sing he'll be home for Christmas,
    I know that's its true—each Christmas you do!!
You're here with me now, you'll ring in the new
    Can't let you forget me, I won't forget you!

You were my buddy, my Daddy, my friend,
    When I was just little, I looked up to you
You held my hand when I went to camp,
    Encouraged me – dried my tears
I wasn't so sad or scared with you there

You told my sister to watch out for me, not really sure if she agreed
    I was OK anyway, I met made friends along the way

Lots of reminders of other nice times :
    You'd throw me and my brothers up in the air
Kinda scary - but we trusted you there

We went on the rides at kiddie-land fair, sure was exciting—a family affair
    Except for Mom, she never did come

You'd play the accordion and sing us some songs
    No TV then, we'd all sing along
You were rather a musical guy - could carry a tune, you'd sing "Blue Moon"

Came home sometimes on Saturday noon
    Swoop us up and dance around the room
We were cleaning and singing, hearing the tunes
    Hearts full of music, loved all the words
Came through from you – instilled somehow

Sensitive souls, pain carried deep, in worlds we could no share
    No sources of comfort—our souls to bare
    So few words spent, here and there

One more thing before I go -
    Not certain if I'll have a lot more time
To speak of things when they come to mind

Thanks to you and Mom for taking me to bingo
    Sharing those treats at the time
We never had won money, but we had other luck -
    The company was quite fine!

I felt on top of the world, when I was hanging with Mom and Dad
    Not a lot far and between,
But some to remember and feel really glad!

I watched the sound of music again this year,
    I'm sure you remember that special day -
You both took me to see it when I was thirteen
    Wow, what a movie, what a treat!
One of the best I've ever seen

Still feels like a dream to me—nice to remember -
    You did that for me, went out of your way
Watching a family so happy and free
    Just sitting there between...my parents and me

You patched up my knees each time I fell, rather quite often – a real tom-boy!
    You cared for me back then, I could tell

Maybe it's easier when we're young - don't have to talk about other bad things
    Just laugh and play and have fun

I never told you in so many ways - I tried to say it in cards and such
    Really don't think that's quite good enough

I want to make sure I tell you right now
    Speak in word and heart – try to summarize
Won't end it too soon, there's more to be said
    To give honor and dignity too, bring you some justice, let it be read

Times like unwrapping gifts under the tree
    Then running to your room to share
Skipping, tripping filled with glee!
    We'd ask if we could have a hug
Felt so safe like a bug in a rug

Were happier times back then - seemed to change before I was 10
    Wish you guys could have been happier too -
Kids don't like to see parents blue

You did a lot with what you had
    Made our lunches and drove us to school
When it was real cold, not too bad for a hard-working Dad

Dad, I hope I've said things in just the right way
    Never meant to hurt you or cause you alarm
Quite sure I did, to my dismay

Just like my knees you tended with caring hands -
    And other life-fractures and things unkind
God has them covered for us both this time!

Oh by the way, thank you for teaching me to care about God and such
    You told me it was important to believe
Good advice, He's given me much!
    Goodness and wisdom, peace – and help that I seek
Especially these words now I'm able to speak!

The gospel music we shared, in our hearts—not far apart
    Too bad you had to move on so soon,
Just like the song "Movin On"

Never spoke my good-byes that last time
    So sorry for that! But I know God would have come…
And picked up the slack

So Dad here goes, a proper farewell
    Leona said you were doing cartwheels in Heaven – this was her dream
Said you were happy and whole, you still had your leg!
    So glad to know your pain is all gone
Your right there in heaven, just where you belong

For all the good things you tried to do
    In all of the music—I listen for you

You know that good, it never dies
    And so Veda Zein for now
We'll meet up soon – you know how time flies!

Like your favorite gospel song - reminds me much about being strong
    Believing in Heaven and Jesus and things
All good things to God belong

So I'll play this song in remembrance of you
    For all of the hardships – the war you went through
I have it on tape, will ring in the new:
    I'll march with you—salute you too
When the SAINTS GO MARCHING IN

p.s. Say hi to Mom, I'll be writing her soon
p.s.s. Oh yes, and I'll try to be good for goodness sakes

Love always, Alice

Fair of Feather

A wide assortment of fair-feathered friends
    Hatched up a plan to travel afar -
A special event they want to attend

Some have flown solo, others in pairs,
    Many have gathered in flocks and have fled
Passing some friends and nodding their heads

Seagulls have come mainly for food
    Foraged by hunters by the sea-bed

No matter the weather, be it fowl or fair -
    All very sprightly up there in the air

They've flown in rotation all set to please
    Some will even float in with the breeze

Announcements went out well in advance,
    Sent messages ahead, some sparrows have said
With pigeons that carried the message it read

Sang songs telling others—the white doves to fly
    All beings a part of a universal sky

Sang it loud, sang it clear:
    "Unite to attend this worldly affair,
Viewing will be conducted outside in the air"

Wide variations of all different songs
    Assortments of colors will be on display -
From all different and fashions of flair

Our bushy-tailed friends are awake and alert
    They've had lots of practice, now lay low and wait
The chorus is ready—to the stage now they take

The God Release

Got their orders from below
    Initiate their shoves and blows

Done my penance, let me go
    No need to further escalate or perpetrate

Don't be part of their crime
    Separate, let go of hate

Too much drama on TV
    No need to let it live in me
Try and find a better fate
    Find the one to Heaven's gate

Make this be your last mile
    On the path of wrath and hate
Where demons live in gloom-filled air
    With spooky eyes that starkly stare
Kind of cold and frigid there

Just friendly ghosts and flying fairies
    Wands that sparkle – stars of light
All are friendly, none are scary

Let goodness be your new-found fate
    You know that soon will be too late
Heaven's gate will close and seal—the other side has locked you in
    No more goodness to reveal

Climb the hill—don't look back
    Take some time to comprehend
No exit button or quick release
    Once you're settled in that part
Only God can set you free

In God's Name

Not a great prelude to my day, the enemy tried to lead me astray
    Irate to see me take my time - find good ways to spend my day

Sole intent—remove me from your sacred space
    So holy and precious this state of grace

Happens less often – a bit wider-spaced, God injects instead his hand of love
    Wants me to wear it—make it fit like a glove

In trying it on I pull and tug – still a bit big
    I'll be patient and wait

Not merely for goodness or goodness sales
    But for the spirit of the Father and His blessed Son

He stepped out of heaven onto this earth, entered within and told us His name
    When we step into heaven he'll claim us again

The Clearing

Their furs are soft, they warm and cover
    … Still some chillness in the air

Some of them are torn and bare
    All the rest—lead me through,
To see the forest in the trees

Their peacefulness speaks to me,
    Although their quiet as can be
They free me as I walk upon -
    Their sure and steady solid ground

Lost some needles – their all around
    Leaves that fell, I trod upon
As I listen to their crunch, I muse on things they give to me

Could go on for miles,
    Walk about and talk about, as they enter me

Open mind, the wind blows through—wanting just to come along
    Although it gusts it stills my thoughts, of silhouettes that linger there

I'll move on through the forest bed and surely by the by -
    I find a patch will open up to see a sky that's clear and blue

Through The Trees

Smell of Spruce surrounding me
    Deep rich aroma – heaven scent, as I walk among the trees

Seasons come and go, all in time with earth's life flow
    Keep their ground won't be moved, standing solid as they grow

Offer much to talk about - their pleasant state accompanies me
    Surround with thoughts and imagery

Come walk with me along its paths
    Through the mighty forest walls – follow them as they call
Their legs are thick – broad and strong, I'll lean on them, their manly girth

Arms stretching out with branches wide, leaves are damp and glistening
    They sway and frolic as they play, rich and full – brimming life
Dressed in leaves of green and gold, such a glory to behold

I hear their rustle through the breeze
    Singing songs of nature calls
Side by side in unison, reaching out to speak to me

Tastes To See

Summers here the trees are full
    Fruits are ready – ripe
Indulgences to entreat and savor

Berries cherries peaches pears
    Sewed and sewn – now to reap
Look so fine, smell so sweet

Grapes of Grace right from the earth
    Opened wide her full-length skirts

Taste them once and you will see
    How very generous God can be

He gave them free and with His Favor
    Blessed us with his gifts of trees

The Messenger

Sweet Jesus comes a thousand different ways
        Many varied things to say
Speaks to all—reaches some

Oh I'm learning quite a lot
        Through different words and thoughts

He's working with his light and power
        Showing me—other ways

That He's the one to lean upon
        His Revelations – weigh a ton

Ancestry's and roles, played before astrologies
        Bent and formed and played
Amazed! Things sent through, unique his way—always new

Strike me somehow instantly—magically
        Deep empowered undertones, resounding long
Like lightening quick – thunder strong

Just sends them in right here and now
        There's no delay, he bursts right through
Can't play around with things like that

Try to look at what's below to talk of light and dark
        .. Many deep things

Of things unknown – untold
        Other worlds of words, things we thought we knew
Linger, vanish, start anew – bringing new mystique

Don't interfere with his story or the way in which its told
        All these little specks of sand, small parts of a greater plan

They're beautiful—profound, stop me speechless; spell-bound
    Cut to the quick, amaze, astound

Sure and steady, he sets the time – two hearts that beat in unity
    Take and taste, stand transfixed. It's magic there!

The Interval

He's the open space – breeze in my hair
    Wind at my back, lightness of air
Snowfall at night cast in the light

Leaves in the trees – branches that bend
    Light-lending stories, stars shining bright
Love that move, tears that cry, — lullabies

Shoes on my feet, walk of the path, love that lasts
    Coat that covers, quietness of mind, sounds of warmth
Stillness of night, moisture of dew, soaking of sun
    Bubbles of bath, children's laugh, eyes of the owl

Lists of life, things that touch to feel and feed, lift and heal
    Oceans of meadows, surrounded by trees, swimming seas, wild life

Meditations of life, can't lose this time – all sitting there
    Willing to share—cast out our rods—sit and wait
Pull in space, catch some divine, nets in full; kind—cast in the mind

Just words I know – their free – energy
    Time to devote, keeps me true – pauses in rhyme, never ends there
Words – always more, to breathe in the air

All these I'm able to speak, given with lips -
    Kiss long and warm, linger and speak
So many words, short and sweet
    Keep in a heart, deep – profound

Read Between The Lines

Things not always as they seem, surface sitting quiet, serene
  No simply not as their seen

Don't really speak to what has been
  You'll find there's been some deeper cracks
Found their ways to get around

Not always open skies safe and clear or welcoming
  Often many stormy seas held them back – left their tracks
Furrowed long wide and deep

Get real close, take a look
  Not really such an open book

Close The Books

Christmas time come and gone
    Still time moves right along

Want to remember some of those moments in time
    Look at them once again, let them jingle here or there
Turn some pages then close the book
    All important, significant - like the words, they live on

Will close the books for awhile but save the page of each of them
    Marked in ink – they won't rub out; find their spot and settle in

Land of Grand

Hey there Mom!

I've think and thunk about ways that I should talk,
    Don't come easy – intricate
Just like to try and make them fit

We tried to reach out sometimes through life's ups and downs
    Never quite touched your pain – nor you mine.
Separate worlds; two different girls

You talked of yore and romance -
    Of days when you and Dad would dance,
Told us stories when we were small,
    In pleasant songs and nursery rhymes

Gave big hugs - I remember then ..
    I felt your love

Saved each little dime you made,
    Always giving pleasant times

At Christmas dashing here and there,
    Choosing every gift with care.
A very thoughtful giving mom

Having fun, young and wild, we ran free
    Back then, so carefree

You tried to keep us treasured souls -
    In your land of ferry dust,
Sprinkled with your warm soft hands,
    To keep us in your merry land

Filled with candy treats and gifts,
    Embraces sweet, remember, keep

The magic you once had - you shared with us to hide the bad
    Of other dreams and story tales, that lived in you and what you knew
All so grand! Left behind when you came, to this new land

Stormy seas and troubled times - instead claimed you.
    Dismantled with the woes of war, came to share and live with you

You kept such heart and fortitude, good strong stock within your kin.
    Though you traveled many a mile, always tried to wear a smile.

Sometimes I'd go up to our attic, try on all the frilly things -
    Frocks and slips, crinolines, pretend I'd live with Princes – Kings
Fancy things – worlds unseen, join with you in fantasy-filled lands,
    Find those times that were so grand!

Merchant's Deceits

Tables are set with all of their wares
    Not meant for the public but still they lay there

Claim their good, decent, fair - make you believe there's nothing that's wrong,
    Draw you to their dance and song.

Make them appear good as new -
    You'll soon find – unfit to view.

They've vendors of evil, wolves at your door, up to no good
    Peddling their own bill of rights -
Never thought you'd look under their hood

Clothes are ill-fitting, source is impure, no interlining, its rough and it tears
    Merchandise is faulty, stained with lies -
Thought they had such a clever disguise

Nothings arranged in an organized way, open or friendly – a messy display
    No quality there too threadbare, can see right through
Crews dishonest, just don't care.

Mouths are smiling as they stare, look at their eyes—they lie too
    Lips are moving, words ring hollow, faces sallow, false, fake
Hard pills to swallow – my leave I'll take

The Potter

I don't need to find God solely in church when he lives here in my heart
    Though won't rule it out,
Been times in past I've looked for him there –
    To settle my soul

Some pieces were missing, others were bare
    Some stuffed and bound – they needed some air

I just want the Potter, wherever he may be
    He says his yoke is easy, his burden is light

Don't need to be pounded to see things your way
    Kinder forces can easily sway

He will not force grasp or grab, only encourage and guide
    He won't ever hurt you or make you feel bad

So many things he's done for us, can't count them all
    You'll see them in time, clear as the sky bright as the sun

Coincidentally

Felt powerful, deep—took my wind
    No chance to stay on your feet
Too profound, intense for words
    God-laden spectacular when spirit fed

Amazing superb dimensions from God
    Their mammoth, they speak
Enlarge – make you want to weep

Enchant, drives heart and soul; gravitates, fixates
    Coming through Christ – born to us
Can't break them down, much too rich – their glory bound

Specialist of Light

He's a visionary specialist, he'll keep you in sight;
    Never go blind if you focus on him,
He's the ocular guy.

Specialization is caring, he has his degree,
    He'll never fail you—watch him and see

Won't give you tests too hard to pass,
    Or let you struggle in dullness or gloom -
He'll reflect through the glass, let you see through

He'll shine His light on you to brighten your day
    Keep you seated when you struggle to see.
He'll be right beside you, a true visionary.

Nothing can cause you to sway or trip,
    He's filled the prescription, written the slip.
He's looked very close, seen through your eyes.
    Won't make a mistake – he's looked down too deep.

Adjusted the lens, corrected the view,
    Brought in a new angle, made old things new.

Action Moves

Laugh with me, cry with me, touch me, lift me, carry me,
    Sing with me, dance with me, walk with me, sit with me.

Smile at me, hear me, listen to me, hold me, feel me, cherish me,
    See me – respond to me.

I don't choose to sleep on – while I lay here awake,
    I'll find and maintain much deeper a state,
In actions words that move and stir.

Don't want to break this sweet little bubble,
    Hangs here with me – taken the trouble.
A zone of contentment and bliss,
    An act and a will that's not hit and miss.

Actions and movements of fun and good sport,
    Energetic and lively to stay with the flow.
Ringing vibrations of health and good cheer,
    Move with the momentum – helps me to grow.

This is the way I'll ring in the new Year
    Fast, to free the bad energy
Let go in time, retrieve the divine

Mainstream was heavy, clogged-impure,
    Disrupted the system – needed a cure.
Cleanse, regenerate; get rid of the old, nourish the new
    Pursue a lighter healthier state.

Stay in sync, move into the zone.
    Don't be resistant, hear the new sounds.
See them in good vibrations of air -
    They're moving quite easy, sure to rebound.

Felt in pockets of earth's synergy;
 Plenty of words out there to share.
Good fuel to stay healthy and help us to thrive,
 Be part of the action to keep us alive.

Deeper Waters

Can't stay in shallow waters, the currents won't flow,
    I need deeper waters to keep me afloat.

Jump into their waves, they'll take you along,
    Their teeming with life swimming so free.
Don't stand at the seashore—come in with me

Leave all your worries behind in the sand,
    Come and see wonders under the sea;
A stunning adventure – you'll soon understand.

Some will be complex – go over your head.
    Rather like seeing a new foreign land -
Stop for awhile, try floating instead.

Then move on ahead - don't look back to the shore,
    After some time it becomes quite a bore.

Hold onto your hat, take the bull by the horn,
    Leave all else behind, new adventures in store.

Lifestream

Stupefied in world and ways,
    Caught up in it's undertows.

Tugging pulling this way and that,
    Tossed me about, my face it slapped.

Tired and weary yet felt compelled -
    To kick right back.

Closed my mouth – too hard to swallow -
    The spit and froth their waves churned out,
Let too much in, it weighed me down.

God told me, "Child, don't struggle so -
    You're much too tense.
Unclench your fists from worldly grips,
    Open up, let them go.
Follow me I'll bring you ease, to streams of life
    Where you can flow."

Light Switch

Look alive, been too long anesthetized -
    Got my ticket paid, pre-planned my trip.

Kept my wits, made the call, message read:
    "There's lots of room in Heavens Beds."
Jesus said, "Your welcome, stay for all eternity."

Glad I read the maps and signs, studied all the story lines,
    Authenticated, verified.

Looked at paths—seemed much too dark,
    Sought some others; scrutinized.
Checked out my heart, The Way felt right -
    Glad I chose the One so bright.

Happy now I'm on my way -
    To leave behind the dull and gray.

Cleansing Time

Hitched up my skirt, hit the dirt.
    Rolled up my sleeves – got to work.

Tried to sweep things beneath the rug,
    Had to dig to clear the air.

Jesus said, "I'll help you sweep, you've played too long.
    These foolish games are now unfit.
You need some new, not many – don't overdo:
    Just enough to see you through.
Clean them up, unstitch the old, wash them out, iron folds

Don't need a new house, you have a home;
    There's lots of supplies the owner left behind.

Won't take too long – a short small skit,
    Clean up the act, will make like new, sparkle – shine.

Gifts of Reason

Knocked around pretty good,
    Emotions raw, badly bruised.

Thank you for your excellence,
    Going all those extra miles, in your most extraordinary way!
Unusual for us—normal for you.

You stuck around, stood your ground,
    Opened up your point of view.

Made things clear when we faltered,
    Kept us steady through the season,
Brought your gifts of rest and reason.

Who needs Santa when we have Jesus?
    Oh mighty God, rock of gibraltar,
Be our reason—in each season.

The New Recruits

They're much too young to be formed with your clay,
    Leave them alone to find their way.

There's still some good crops for them to sew;
    Don't throw toxins to clog their roots -
Already dying from poison they've had,
    Will just bring them down to sink in the bog.

The world needs people to set things right,
    They're topsy and turvy and crooked enough.

Nurture their talent and guide them in truth.
    They have the will, let them begin.

Many good things to do—let it start with you.

The Plaintive Calls

Listen, but don't be alarmed with their cries,
>They come from afar, but pierce the night air.

They're trying to rouse you and sing you their song,
>In hopes you will hear them and show that you care.

Become rather restless – now take in hand ;
>To try to restrain you from killing their land.

Invading their people, and robbing them too -
>From all that they worked for and all that they do

They've been there so long, ages in time;
>Respected and nurtured – made peace their stand.

They don't mean to harm you – just like you, they want to be free
>They'll help you and heal you with plants they have grown

Enriched by the soil, they've nourished by hand.

There's all kinds of room and plenty of space -
>Don't rape or pillage, or cause them disgrace.

We're all a part of God's human race.

They hoot and they holler but don't cast them out,
>Their dance is their song to give God His praise

Their fire is meant to embrace, welcome and warm you, encircle with grace.

Put your weapons aside, be peaceful and kind,
>Join in the circle to celebrate life -

No longer to hear the cries in the night,
>But wailing's of joy – shouting delight.

Glow With Christ

I have hearts in my eyes.
    Embers glowing fires of red.

I'm being refined and loving this time.
    Radiates his commitment and promises – lures.
Draws ever near to brighten my days.

I know that the Father's drawn Jesus to me,
    There's no mistaking his face that I see.
I read it in corners and spaces he frees.

I need to do business solely with him -
    He'll honor and seal – extract from my will.
No hidden costs, investment is sure.
    He has the resources, he always fulfills.

All Godly treasures, no limits in mind,
    Shiny as silver, solid as gold.

I'll try to stay on the path he lit,
    It's teeming in richness, radiating love;
Always brings sunshine no matter the time.
    Transformed by His goodness, enshrined in his mind.

Illuminating glare, he'll leave with you there ...
    To flicker and flare.

In The Name Of God

Supposed christians are full of deceit -
    They wear God's cloak,
But their deceitful offenses are the worst crime of all.

Faces veiled with lace and frills,
    Look straight in your face, never blinking an eye,
Smile with their eyes and hiding their lies.

Their the ones you should trust, say God's on their side
    Whatever they do He'll surely abide -
Just so profound the harm they can do,
    All the while they profess they're still beng true.

God says in His scriptures, "Don't strike your neighbor in secret."
    That's why its so hurtful when they do it to you.

I fall to the floor, I'm felled and I'm slain.
    They're hurting their brothers while saying your name.

The sayers have come and impeded your view,
    When their words and their doings do not reflect you.
God I know there's only so much you can do.

So sad to see others stumble and trip -
    They'd heard about you, these lambs of your flock,
Lost in their way, were blinded and strayed.

Despite the disguise I looked straight through;
    Looked very hard, from your point of view.
So very different, but your way is real
    I'm happy to say—I know the real You.

Imprints

They've all been silenced a long time ago
    Never to claim, or be given a name
At least not on earth, but always by God

He says He has them in the palm of his hand
    They'll never be lost, can't separate or part

He'll hold them for you throughout each new year
    He's tended to them, called them his friends
He heard when they cried, picked them up when they fell

Carried them through, made him their home – knows their real names
    Their proper and regal and dignified too
You'll recognize them, they're cousins to you

You wont need a copy, you carry the print
    Their entitled Emmanuel, it means "God with you"
It's embedded in you

Your part of their seed that nourished their soul
    Can never disguise them or cause them to hide
They fit and belong – part of heart's whole
    He brings us all home to have and to hold

Lasting Impressions

Talk about Jesus, He's not their reason
    Got their own special logic, different from the road he trod
Live more for the festive season
    Incrementally measured – always weighed

Shifts around from day to day, inspect you – compare to us
    I'll pray for you, look down on you, see you – then I'll look away

Speak to you, kneel and pray, step on you, help you, hurt you, lie – betray
    Which part of Jesus did you neglect,
When you slayed me with your disrespect

Heard your voice in the hall, soft, sweet, pale -sallow
    Ringing out, hollow, shallow
Need to make the transference, don't step in – then step out
    Illuminate the Jesus feel, make it fit – make it real

Take Them In

You may have passed this way before and saw my fruit
    Stayed to play and picked a few
They're from the same family tree, with their own distinctive tastes

Recognize their shapes and forms, seen by many different factors -
    Digestive tracts are quite reactive

Don't rush about with them, sit and savor
    They're all prescribed to bring good health
Friendly foods with taste and flavor

Pause and wait – take some time, soon to flow and move on through
    Don't worry about how they come out, he takes care of all loose ends

Digest them all, reuse, re-cycle - don't let them all go to waste
    One's left over may be refined, suited for some other tastes

That's alright – they'll all be used, quite hardy, not easily bruised
    Digestible, acceptable – compatible

Words of Play

Fun to think about, twist – puzzle about
    Roust and joust, get into the act, interact

Frolic, sway, write about, set apart, inter-mix, split apart
    Dance or sing with them, throw about, pray about
Keep – enfold, or give away

More precious than gold, ours to have and hold
    From God when he spoke the word, then Jesus came to make it heard

Took and turned them inside out - each time you try to touch and name
    They'll play with you and say, "I'll hide, come seek" -
Then show up in a whole new way!

This play is fun, makes you want to leap and run
    Especially Jesus' part – instrumental—detrimental
Written recorded read and rhymed, played and scripted for all time

Give a toast, "Cheers to him"! Offer precious thanks and hymns
    Speak the words blessed by love
That cleansed and washed away our sins

Foods For Life

Hey my family here and there, wish you were around today
    You'd so enjoy the soups and stews
You didn't always eat enough, needed more goodly stuff

Guess I'll enjoy myself, think of you when I eat my food
    Pray that your all healthy too

My heart misses you sometimes, fills with sadness and regret
    I want to pay you my respects

Please stay well and happy too. Rest in peace.
    I'll think of you along the way, I keep you in my heart – for you I pray

The Uniforms

My mother let me be a brownie—a highland dancer too
    I loved all the pockets, the tie and the belt
I think there was a badge too, it made me feel so proud
    I wore it quite vainly, because I was allowed

A rather fine spectacle a girl—in all that garb!
    I think there was also some type of cool cap -
I sure do remember how good it felt

Not sure how we afforded – the money was tight
    I guess I was important to them alright!
Why did I not know it or feel it back then?
    It could have all been a game of pretend

Sure was kind of fun though, I liked all the dancing
    The hops and jumps, the whirls and twirls
Made a young girl – feel happy and light!

Thanks for the memory of those happy days
    They sure bring back sights for sore eyes
A wee girl so free, dancing all around -
    Wearing a kilt with so many pleats
Held together with a big shiny pin

Wish I could press them and tuck them away,
    Look back to them to smile and grin -
Perhaps in a scrapbook for the good olden times

They seem to be safe in my memories for now – touch wood!
    I may write them down—perhaps in a book?
They'll keep there forever, for anyone who cares to open and look

Tried and True

We all just want to be like people, unpretentious and true
    Be part of a circle warmly embraced
Sit down at the end of the day, share a nice meal – say how you feel
    Maybe not talk at all, yet still feel that embrace

No fighting or fretting to cling to the air,
    To cause such discomfort worry and care
This is a time to pass stories around
    Laughter and lightness for everyone to share

We all know each other – everyone's name
    I just call them family, I know they're my friends
The waters been tested, it's pure and it's clear
    Can go ahead and drink it without any fear

They've examined the contents, they know the real you
    Even the rough stuff—walked some with you
Lifted each other on days that were blue
    Your pain and your sorrow – they also knew

There's been trials, I admit that is true
    Been lots of tensions we've had to sort through
And bring some attention to some of our cares

It's made us some stronger no matter the stakes
    Look around the circle—it's love on their face

Just Shout Hallelujah

Get on the ball, don't delay or forestall
    Catch the beat, join along – sing Glory, Glory
Winters here – nothings bleak, got my God on this side

His Karma's good enough for me, my driving force
    Just get me up on that Jesus train!
People stopped using that line,
    Said it took too long - slowed them down

Me, I like the open road, so much to sing about
    Unshadowed, unshaded – unparalleled glee
Solitude thoughts in His restful stops, bible sitting on my knee

Lots of time for every word, every page marked with a star
    You are active worship, no need to look too far
Beyond telling—indescribable, inexpressible -
    Celebratory, out-swelling joy!

Been just too selfish, hoarding its call -
    My party with awe, enthralled with it all!
Fiery fireworks, shooting like stars, eclipsing, surrounding,
    Revolving the moon

You in Your Word, alive, - jumping around – ready to play
    There in the morning – starting my day
Can never outsmart you – much too clever and coy
    Atrociously funny, can play with but not toy

Enamor and swoon, come in or exude
    Quicken my pulse, or adjust it to slow
Make time to run or call out the sun

Everything wonderful, use them for good
    Just shout out—don't sit and wait—get up, celebrate!
Say rah, rah! Worthy to be praised – stun and amaze
    Let me confess, I'm bursting with pride
Look to your face, your halo – it's rays!

Clap your hands, lift in praise, dance to his music
    Sing - "What a prize, what a King"
Make use of this time I bring here to mind

Alpha, Omega, once and for all; Everlasting Father, Prince of Peace,
    Creator Elohim - all names in in His hymns
Sing Hallelujah Jehovah – Raah, the Lord is our Shepherd
    Let them be heard!

Just Go To God

I hear the whooshing, blowing and hissing,
    Spitting, whirling and gusting;
Tumbling and thrashing and scurrying around

Let it play out – go with it and sit with it,
    Tap with the flow – scamper with them.
Don't look out to it, don't need to know.

Got it's own reason, I just let it go ..
    Sit here and rest.

In my own season now in this space
    Not caught up in weather making it's case
Chilly out there, warm in this place

I think it's o.k, not always will fit
    It's sized up by God to geographically sit
He's stirring the pots
    Some will be hot, some just lukewarm

God meets me here time after time-
    Enters within my little cocoon
Very pleasant, enough room to move,
    Can snuggle and share, got my best friend there

Went out and invited and welcomed him in
    He left all the pots to simmer and sim
Everything's holy and blessed to Him

Red Flags

Red means stop you've reached the end
    You should have read the signs back then

They were trying to speak to you
    Alert you to the dangers there

Guess they weren't big or hold enough
    Their brightness shaded by the sun

I saw too many clouds along the way
    Rain and snow dimmed the day

View too harsh land too rough
    Couldn't find the strength to stay

Missed the mark - the trail marked "Finish"
    Ran around the circuitous route

Lost my steam - all worn out
    Lost my guide, threw in the towel
Got stuck right there

Stopped awhile-took some time
    Found my guide, my source; bought his map

Marked the place where I got lost
    Led me on a safer path

The Unspoken Word

I'd like to speak and vocalize
    These things I'd say :

Don't persecute, bully, hit me - torment me
    Don't violate me - don't touch me there
I'm not yours to hurt and punch,
    I'm all God's to love a bunch!

Instead I might just not speak
    Unspoken word is sometimes heard -
By your shadows as they pass
    May sit sometimes, surrounding me
I think I see some substance there -
    Comes from somewhere inside

A place that's soft - light as air
    May reflect some personhood
Not so clear and visible -
    But still I feel it's feathered touch

Don't say a word - please be kind
    Don't have to talk or change my mind
Keep me company for awhile
    Don't disappear or leave too soon
Leave the bud with the bloom

If you've seen me when you leave
    Please take away these other things
There much too harsh - their blinding me

And when you flee this dark and see some sun
    Perhaps they'll shrink and fade away

Then I'll be o.k. - much lighter then
    I'll be heard
Won't have to say a single word

War Games

This is warfare pure and simple, see the demons as they play
    Playgrounds rife with satan's boys,
They're all set up they're well-endowed
    Crime for them, it sure does pay

Wont cost too much to join the game, you'll be paid back in spades ..
    All you do is sell your soul and meet them in the town of Hades

Come and join them in their fray, they're just about to ruin your day
    They're fed, instructed, stocked and armed
Funded by their Uncle Sam, they're all kin - their family

Like to claim their talented - resourceful, witty, mischievous
    All good fun, no harm - no foul, can't they see their full of sin?

They use words to cover - hide
    Can't disguise, they're weak they're thin

Not so sly - truth wont ride, God's transparent - he never lies
    Eye's see clear - far and wide,
Slippery feet wont stand, they'll slide
    Soaked and muddy, slip and creak, flip-flop and twist
This their chosen path to keep

They'll walk with you - talk with you, even try to know your name
    Dont let them tag along too long,
Just let them pass - they don't belong

Their cloak and daggers are for real, not just naughty boys at play
    This is war - their not just toys, fully ready to deploy

Cold and empty mercenaries, hurt and kill - rob and steal
    Conscience stripped - naked, bare: watch their empty steely stares

Quite the family - quite the breed, all just puppets, on a string
    Pulled by men - playing Kings

Don't be touched with words of guise, they're just muted shadowed lies
    Tainted flowers - compromised

Let them slip and slither through; although their bigger then they seem
    Their potent, harmful - if you take them in

Look at their list and their background
    Shine the light - shine it strong
True names there, they glare - their stark
    Their counterfeit, their cheap, they're all mis-fits

Review the list:

Talented, resourceful, witty, mischievous

Not mischievous	-	devious
Not witty	-	cruel
Not talented	-	corrupt
Not resourceful	-	calculated

Not misguided, but mislead; they'll lose you in their strategy

Really not such a healthy list - you'll need to focus and resize:

Not innocent clever or discreet, undercovers crooked, warped
    Inlays faded, mismatched and blurred

Lists are not short and sweet, may seem small - insignificant
    Meant to entertain and sway your mind,
Hope you'll simply look away

Not Schindler's list your looking at, won't help or stay you -
    Look at them, give full review, don't be misled with what they said

You can't deflect, their not secure - they wont protect
    They'll set you up, they'll throw your guard,
Brain wash you, sedate you and put you to sleep

Stay awake, hold your line, don't live in that place of war
    Get out of that combat zone, you're in too deep
See through them, seek peace, don't let them blind you I implore!

Have Faith

He's so funny, brilliant too
    I thought I'd write a poem or too two

He said, "I'm surprised you chose so few,
    You think I'd curb this abundance for you?"

How little you know, what small faith you do show!
    You've seen my credentials, you know full well what I do!

Grab in handfuls, let them show, take a bunch, run and use
    You know it's a race you cannot lose!

Look At My Face

It all shines through your eyes - makes me alive
    See through the tunnel, the vastness of me
Touches, stills - without lifting a hand

There's intimacy there, I feel I know it quite well
    It's personal - not obscure in any way
Influential, heartfelt, friendly - rises to greet

Won't shade my eyes though your light is quite bright
    Just want to stay - transfixed with you there

Too sacred to move or take a new stance
    Your vision is piercing - in awe I just stare
Just keeps me seeking, suppresses all cares

New will has surfaced in iron-clad light
    It's focused on purpose
The rainbows and rays will help keep me stayed

It's My Party

We're here together, sharing this day
    He's my birthday present

It's thrown in His Honor, he frosted the cake!
    Can sing Hallelujah, in sync or alone
Carefree in nature, sing high or low

Don't need a whole lot of people around
    Won't bring me down or make me feel sad
I want to be lifted, I want to feel glad!

Born again today I celebrate my life
    Always the same - from your point of view
Feeling my joy from my head to my toes!

I invited some others to share in my joy -
    They never showed up, they missed all the fun!
He says its o.k, though if I want to cry

Who do you really say that I am?
    Not really a name - just a heart that is new
Been christened in favor, a part of his plan

Sometimes one friend is all that you need
    To help blow the candles, make your wishes come true

I see you're still there - though it's late in the day
    Candles still burning, light is still bright
You heard all my wishes, main ones come true
    I'm happy to see you're still here in sight

Connections

Long flowing legs
    Eyes looking at you - watch their eyes

Step into the moment - no need to speak
    There's truth lying there, stark, bare
Won't let me touch . . delve into deep
    Only to dance and play with you there

Can only intrigue so fixed it's allure
    Crafts hidden magic will cut you in half - unhinge and surprise
Uncanny divisions, fragments of heart
    Struck by the beauty that makes you feel whole

Curvaceous flirtations - waves in the air
    Lips that will linger, lush-deep
No lies to tell you no need to speak
    Already captured, sunk in too deep

Meant only to hold enthrall and entrance
    To stir in your soul and languish in love
Compelling it's call - to go out and meet

Soft-spoken language may teach you some things
    Aroused in it's passion, let them stand still
Connections that live in life's hidden things

Overflows

The list goes on day after day, no more restraining or keeping at bay
    It's your turn to speak you've much to say

Been shoved in the background stemmed up too long
    No doors sitting open to get out and move

Seems no catching up or stopping the flow
    Currents are bursting and spilling their seams
Crammed in the corners are seeking release

You said, "That's enough, now is the time - pull out all stops
    Open your arms, there's rivers of blessings now here to flow

They'll cover the places starving and parched
    I'll release them and free them - just let them grow!
Treasures reaped up for all who have sewn

Now you have found Me, I'll bring you in front
    Come here beside me, Me I won't let you go"

The Bully's Points

Had outnumbered 10- 1, still they brought in—more big guns
    Must have looked like easy preys, gave them time to gather – play

Continual harassment, prolonged distress
    Is what you'll see – should you confess
Don't even try to name their names
    They'll set you up, they'll give you stress

Jesus hurry, get here quick!
    There getting ready – to place more kicks
All their pals have gathered round, this craziness is much too sick
    Their all eager, so ready to bring you down

Can't think of better games to play - this one causes calamity
    Must be blinded, can't they see—don't they care?
Their victims wounds, raw and blistered
    Exposed and festered by your stares

What bent their minds, what fueled their rage,
    That prompted them to play this game

Not civilized or pure clean fun, in fact it's rather quite insane
    Intentional – to shame and blame, cruel and lame – a real fool's game
Where weaker minds are so inclined

Can't you see God's handiwork, there in his face and in his eyes
    He has a heart, just like you, he has a place – he cries too

Be a force to reckon with, don't turn your head the other way
    Or just sit back and let them pick
Shroud him from their glares of hate, hold his hand and foster love
    Lead him to a safer place, give him back his state of grace

It's a struggle – I know it's hard, to hone some skills and look inside
    Nerves of steel are buried deep, long been hidden – gone to sleep
Fought with worry and with doubt

May have to try and seek some others help
    Hope their true and real heartfelt
Maybe find a different crowd, or better yet – your own true self
    That's good and strong, not easily swayed

Bully's darts are full of poison -
    Viewers sometimes tag along
Sometimes their darts will hit you too
    Get slanted, sometimes their skewed
May turn and set their sights on you
    Vicious circle all around – it never ends

Lot's of ways to look at things, try and find the better view
    Step away, get apart, from hurtful cruel and angry hearts

We'll all be wounded in this way
    Help them – get them on their feet, then turn around and step away
May make tomorrow a better day

In God's Good Time

Don't let discouragement set on your face
    Do you think it's too late – didn't hear the call?
Got the wrong address, zip-code or state?
    No – you've made the right moves, don't worry at all!

Plenty of time to ready yourself
    Don't just sit around on the shelf
He's waiting for you to open the door
    Just outside – there in the hall

He's been hangin around for quite a long time
    He's willing and patient, make no mistake!
He's good and he's God, what more can I say?

Wants to be sure your well on your way
    You won't be afraid if you open the door
All of that brilliance might blow you away!

He's looking for goodness that's packed up with you
    So practice will help you, make sure that you do

Don't be alarmed with any delays - he's always on time
    Don't rush so fast, he knows the right way
Work out your faith, practice your mind
    Open the door; you're on the right path, you're in the right state!

Tempest's Brew

Been engulfed by angry foaming seas, and wrestled with the winds
    Accomplices in unison, using force to bring me down
They seem to be winning, pinning me – won't let me move
    Circling me, blowing round

I'm catching their drifts; they're winding, spurring each other on
    Forces to reckon, got their minds set
Unleash their fury, won't divide or separate – won't relent

Set firmly in place – stretched out and ready to form and stay
    I'll dig in my heels and press on my oars
I too, like them, won't be swayed

Won't let capsize or easily upset, I'll look to my maker and give it my best
    My voice of reason and respect

They may cause me some delay – some masts are shorn
    Though thrown around, the hulls intact
Won't waste my breath, I'll turn my back
    Look ahead to God—he'll get me through

Come In

Go to that place today Jesus – meet me at the gate
    Make all those little snowflakes, arise and elongate

Some may look the same as they surface in the air
    That house out there, it isn't mine, it's separate in its state

The pictures through the mists .. all take their own forms
    Trees different sizes colors, shapes
Their mighty power... not shrouded by the night

Expressive there, invites my look, see all the pictures differently
    Like the clover overlooked, or that bird, on its perch

They don't escape me now, found floating free or standing still
    They move my mind and stir in me, form around ...new backgrounds

Bird atop a cross of stars hung with garlands lying horizontally
    Sideways twists, fresh and crisp – flowers bloom

Clovers leafs sit in orange-hued flares
    Behind there's violet strips of snow filled air
In blue and yellow clouds out there

This page I see within this book, I know its special – unique to me
    Stop to take a second look, arches round to bring you near
It's pictures life, - its awfully clear

Not sure why I never saw before
    Always been there behind those doors

Artificial Flavors

I took a bite, the taste was off – wasn't quite the same
    Acquired taste? Possibly ..
I like the flavor and the zip

Usually comes with a cost – price reflects the quality
    I've tried to skimp so many times
By choosing lesser, cheaper things
    Now I know what value brings!

God said, "Look around and shop, don't rush and grab just anything
    Take some time, stand in line
Wait – I'll bring you wholesome things"

Pretty Colors

God I love all these pretty colors you made
    I know they're from You
They cast and reflect Your shimmering view

Radiant hues tap soft at my door
    I welcome them all
To sit in their rays, soft and light in my heart

Shades of blue in purple twilights
    Pink and white - yellows so bright
So much warmth to enjoy!
    What a sparkling array from a glorious God

I love all these things colored by hm in rich undertones
    Speaks fondness for me from a deep scarlett heart

Set In Place

He's pitched his forks here and there
    Far and wide the swaths cut deep, footholds slip - my feet won't keep

Jesus said, "Don't worry I'm close, right over here,
    I'm the one whose face you seek
Plant your feet and dig in deep,
    You'll find much steeper roads ahead"

I'm standing here watching you, calm and still with love so true
    I wont be moved - I care too much,
I still have strength to lead you through

It's My Word your seeking out, finding ways to spread about
    The lechers miffed - sunk in his teeth, wants to drain your energy

Venomous fangs will cut and seep, aims to siphon good things out
    God knows his plans, he's seen them all, knows the guy - his traits
Shirt-tails still hanging out, tails still long - hateful face

Keep your pace don't be deterred, apostle Paul too, knew his hate
    Thrown in jail - he'd been impeached

You'll be delayed but won't be stopped, his words alive, they jump and hop
    See - there on the bottom line; fixed and true they're there to stay
Fresh and real like all good crops; dont be saddened or dismayed -

He's followed you with new detours, you know his tricks - his lures
    Tempt you then cast you down, twists and turns things all around
Changes words, omits a lot, never gives the real true cost -
    Always tries to get you lost

Apostle Paul's the guy to know - don't buy their other stories; all lies
    They're not the same: It's he to follow – emulate
Keep the pace, its not a race

Sure and steady – can't stop my words, only wind around a bit,
    Skirt on by that short detour, I'm still right here – crystal clear

Follow me, wont lead astray or trip you up, I'll stay with you
    Give you rest and keep you blessed

All the things you set in place, sought for good and did invest -
    They're still right here in safekeeping, locked up in my treasure chest
Always more in store-for he who comes to seek My Face

The Reason

I write poems to stay in peace, I like to feel tranquility
    Awful many things it brings, jingle there to start each day

May be a song I've just heard or a word there in my head
    Lot's of memories – lots of love - regrets and sorrows

    ... Many things

No reason really to stop his words – his plans for me
    I listen, then I just go along

At times some answers to my prayers – find me there
    Dreams too will come alive, their beauty touch
Awaken me, enliven me; speak sweet and fair

    … With their purpose and their reasons

Won't rationalize or justify or make up lies
    Look them up in my heart: they feed – like manna

… God can only be the reason

They narrow in, exhale and breathe; take away a world of clutter
    Crooks and crannies sweetly seasoned

… Miracles of God – their reason

Empty Spaces

Poetry is where I go when I'm feeling low – my tonic tone to soothe my soul
    Dries my tears I cry inside; sometimes they're visible, they seep outside

Their swelling now, I feel them grow – can't tend them now I have to go
    Then I'll sit and speak in rhyme, to all those things that come to mind

These friendly little word attacks, sneak on up throughout my day
    They want to rest or stir my soul; come in part to make me whole

Fills this space that lives with me, I think its only love it needs
    Got its hooks in me – wont let things be; like a fix – I need

Its healthy, it wont mess me up; it's of God, it's all good stuff

Passing Ships

Sometimes I sit and think of them, maybe reach or share a touch
    Find some things to smile about -

        Just a little sister-kin
        Like brotherhood, say "sister-ship"

Perhaps we might go for a walk, read a poem, share some thoughts
    Of tender moments, time long-lost; watch a show, eat some food
Speak of things we'd like to know – all just flesh and blood you know

Time to find life's finer things, feel some sun upon our face
    Fair-winds blow south – through our hair
Lighten earthly stings, spaces heavy, full of care

Sing some sentimental songs – there must be smiles and laughter there
    Some cares and fun to borrow from, reach to find some good to share
I see them float across the shores, in the distance – far away

In His Grace

Heard the whooshing felt the breeze
    In that moment in that church – felt so much!

All that time I searched for him, now see him plain
    He's walking through all my pain

Inhaled his scent of whiteness there; sang in the music, felt in the air
    They said to come – find blessings sure,
Held my breath - were miracles too!

Filtered strong and heavy light, shed all doubt
    Healed my sight

His heart just opened – let me in
    His grace much bigger than all my sins

His cures are real – they help you heal
    His special touch is everywhere
He showed up then – now back again

Good God

A privilege to know him again, got lost in the clouds back then
    Fought and clawed to push them back; found Him on that beaten track

Hold onto him don't let him go,- look high and low
    More precious than any gold

He'll bless you with a kiss, transform you like a butterfly
    Bring you up to greater things – good heavens, he captured me!

Joined the ranks – didn't think I'd made the list
    Am honored just to know his name

Now I'm flying on his shoulders,
    Need to grow some good strong wings
Takes some practice to be a soldier

Zig-zag a bit to find good winds to keep me steady
    Sail me through

Relocation

Dreamed of you my old sweet beau – still pretty as could be
    Just wanted to kiss you kiss you kiss you, kiss
Beauty of dreams-true hearts are red, stay the same yet fonder grow

I saw you in that favorite spot – nothing out of place
    No lines of age; there you sat – smooth as day
Sweet and fair – jet black hair, all seemed to fit

Stood outside looking in – as you walked by -
    Seemed to know where I reside . .

Nonchalant your point of view
    Not off course – our hearts still knew

Leapt in joy – but still . . no big romance just steady – sure,
    There you stood – strong

Yes, I see you though I hide; I know you'll find me anyway
    Afraid to go, afraid to stay – choice in part, mine to play
Already there, invited in – just stay
    Love doesn't need a voice, doors been open all the time

Dream Intents

Why in dreams is love real, so intensely perfect, whole?
    See deep and simple holy souls

Is it God we're seeking out? Has he been there all the time?
    Is he there in part or whole? Is he the root and all-just cause?

Rests in the day – rises nights?
    Maybe too many obstacles to block His path -
Makes us fight to find His light?

Many questions, many stories – all part of my reveries ..
    Still I try to speculate, of what it all might mean to me

Why must we struggle so to seek its love so far and wide?
    . . So deep inside; - questionable, variable

Yet there it is, still and sure – Creation!
    I'll grab it from its source as I can to bridge my sight
My creator tries to make it visible to touch
    So I just say, "Thank you – love you so much!"

Reunite

They say good true friends cannot be lost, cannot be bought at any cost
    Good old souls, heartfelt hearts

Traveled roads much the same, different times – same pilgrimage
    Met up at the same old place

Never docile, always active, give you hope – give you favor
    Try to touch with grace and tact, let you know with kindly acts
Never let you rue the day, you shared your secrets – they stay

Sit and watch those tears you weep, see their eyes – misty too
    They know why; they cry with you

Sit by you, carry through, connect their light
    Share it when its shining bright
Unite with you, feel for you, help you when you lose your sight
    Try to rouse you, see you through

Just some of the things they do
    Good old pals, good old chums

Get Real

Make sure you get to God, even if you have to plough and bow
    Every inch along the way . .

Get on your knees, scratch and claw – this is all just earthly stuff
    Through scrapes and tears – give no care
Knuckle down, stay real; he'll make you hardy – tough!

1st to the end gets a prize! Nothing booby for entering in,
    It's real, its big, it's multi-sided!
Almost like a hexagon – nothing like I've seen before
    It's part of God's anatomy, can only see in his homeland

Don't worry, it's all for real! All quite smooth – homogeneous
    Not just part of the scenery, it's made by him – authentically!
You'll see him when you reach the end… he lives and breathes
    The Real McCoy – The living truth

I know your keen to claim the victory!
    Watch the signs as you tread and shuffle
Soon enough you'll be redeemed!